Communities
of the
Erewash Valley

Times Past and Present

Harry Riley and Brian Fretwell

This 3rd Volume Book / Digest is dedicated
to the Memory of Bill Gregory

Introduction by Harry Riley

Following on from volumes 1 and 2, Brian Fretwell and I decided to drop
'Eastwood' from the title and spread our wings to cover much more of the
Erewash Valley, incorporating Long Eaton, Ilkeston, Kimberley, Cossall
and Awsworth, Eastwood, L/Mill and Heanor, and any other 'appealing
and true' community story coming in from the Valley Residents. Always
bearing in mind that the River Erewash, which rises in Kirkby in Ashfield
and joins the River Trent at Long Eaton, and from which the valley takes
its name, has long been the traditional border between Nottinghamshire
and Derbyshire.

Wherever possible the tales that are submitted to this 'digest' are re-typed / and printed with as little editing by me (Harry Riley) to protect the written integrity of the storyteller and spellings, and it is possible grammatical errors may occur from time to time. However in Book Two, incorrectly I labelled a photo of D.H.Lawrence's companion as his German wife when in fact it was his sister. D.H. L. lovers please accept my apologies for that.

Also, whilst we give as the title of this book: 'Communities of the Erewash Valley,' for our own and hopefully our readers interest and delight, we may stray into surrounding districts, including the glorious Amber Valley making very loose and tenuous connections, and sometimes no connections at all, and not neccessarily in any specific order of sequence (each story has equal value in our eyes.

Finally, please enjoy, dip in and out of this abstract, **'Pick and Mix'** digest, and don't expect formal chapter headings, continuity of dates, or the usual book formatting, as we insert stories and their related photo's as we get them-newspaper-digest fashion. However to maintain a little formality this third digest is divided into four approximately equal parts.

We are indebted to the generous help from Jessica Steege of 'County-Care-Independent-Living' for her proof-reading services and to Stephen Page of 'eeZee-it company' for his additional computer editing and technical 'Mac' support (with all three books in this series of community digests). And to iT2 for providing paper and printing ink supplies. Thanks also to Tony Harper, our Eastwood and Nottinghamshire County Councillor, for generously providing funding for Eastwood Schools to receive all three sets of books in this series, so that future generations may benefit from the importance of local lives and local/social history.

Although these 3 volumes are of a larger size than is usual, and the print and line spacing too is slightly larger and wider we have done this deliberately so that our more mature readers do not have to struggle to read the text. We feel this should help our younger readers, some of whom may be dislexic. This format has been generally well received, otherwise we would not have continued with it and would have returned to the more normal size. However we have experienced an occasional whinge from someone who complained there are too many white spaces on some pages. Since readers are not being charged extra for this we make no appologies. We are grateful for the continued support from all our article contributors and wish to thank them all.

Living by the Erewash Canal

By Sheila Taylor of Erewash Writers

I moved to my house several years ago, particularly because of the canal at the bottom of the garden. It is a constant delight with interesting wildlife: swans, ducks, moorhens, geese, herons, kingfishers and colourful dragonflies. Brightly painted narrowboats pass by frequently with the boaters giving a friendly wave. The canal was completed in 1779, stretching for nearly 12 miles from the River Trent to Langley Mill, with 14 locks, rising 109 feet, being dug in less than 20 months at a cost of £21,000.

Eventually railways were used as a more convenient form of transport for goods such as coal, and in 1968 'The Transport Act' declared the Erewash Canal closed for navigation. At this time there were proposals to fill in parts of the canal but a group of enthusiasts made up of boaters, fishermen, walkers and those who lived and worked along its length, banded together and formed the Erewash Canal Preservation and Development Association.

Volunteers in this association have worked constantly over the years since then. They have restored the great Northern Basin at Langley Mill, this being opened in 1973. Over 4000 tons of spoil were excavated from the basin. 200 foot of new concrete retaining wall was built and a swing-bridge, out of use since the 1930's was renovated. The Grand Opening and Rally of May 1973 was a huge success, attended by 4000 people and 70 boats from all parts of the waterway system. The Lock Cottage at Sandiacre, the last remaining on the canal was threatened with demolition. After a long battle the cottage was saved to become the headquarters of the ECP and DA. Since1991 the cottage has been open to the public and could be visited once a month. The volunteers have restored it, adding furnishings and artefacts in keeping with its long history. This is now a popular attraction for boaters and especially cyclists and walkers with the establishment of the 'Erewash Trail.'

I have enjoyed living in such a beautiful location and being associated with a group of amazing people.

Sheila Taylor.

Harry Riley's note:

There will be much more about the Erewash canal later in this book as it plays such an integral part in the lives and ecology of the valley. It is also very fortunate that the canal has been constantly revised and maintained over so many decades and continues to be a viable resource for country loves, walkers and leisure craft, and all thanks to the sweat and toil of countless volunteers, giving up their valuable time.

(Stories from Kimberley and district, Nottinghamshire)

Richard Shaw Remembers...

As a child I looked forward to school holidays when I was allowed to go to work with my dad. The Shaw family have a very long history in the building trade and I wanted to be a part of that. However my dad said he didn't want me getting my hands dirty and I was 20 before I managed to persuade him to let me join. I worked for 24 years at Shaw Bros, until the recession of 1992/3 left us devoid of cash and we were forced into liquidation.

If it were possible to go back I would be first in the queue: poor money, filthy working conditions, out in terrible weather conditions and hard work but so rewarding.

Even now I see things that I built or maintained as I walk around this area. Unfortunately one of those is the Brewery at Kimberley. We did all their maintenance and repairs both at the brewery and at all the local pubs.

Before Broxtowe Borough Council was formed we worked for the Basford Rural District Council on many local council estates and on the local roads. The biggest estate is the Larkfields Estate and for 3 years after we finished working there the tenants would still ring to see when we were going to do their repairs. We gave up this work because Broxtowe wouldn't pay the going rate at the time. We also stopped doing school-work and railways-work. Perhaps we had put all our eggs in one basket at the brewery.

My father and grandfather before him were very proud to tell people that Shaws built most of Kimberley, especially Newdigate Street: Victoria Street: Noel Street to name but a few. Unfortunately this tradition started around 250 years ago and finished on the 18th January 1993. Family businesses seem to be a thing of the past, sadly never to return.

Harry Riley's note:

This story was reprinted from a community magazine co-edited by Cherry Chance and I.

Watnall is adjacent to Kimberley, and after giving a talk on The Pentrich Revolution and also hunting for local stories/anecdotes in Kimberley Library, Brian and I met a resident who had a very interesting tale to tell concerning World War Two… He is a local historian and here is the story:

'WATNALL, WE KNOW YOUR SECRET…'

Watnall 's WW11 German Spy *by Roger Grimes.*

Watnall was the home of WW11, Fighter Command Headquaters,

officially known as RAF 12 Group H.Q and it was located in two deep bunkers.

Construction of the first bunker, the control centre commenced in 1938. It is situated beneath the raised grass area at the side of the Vehicle Testing Station and was completed in 1940.

The second Operations Centre and the Filter Block, were built in a railway cutting beside Common Lane, currently a construction site, this was not completed until 1943.

Watnall tracked the direction and speed of German bombers as they approached the East Coast, from information relayed by the Observer Corps and Coastal Radar. Fighter aircraft were then scrambled from their Lincolnshire bases to intercept the invaders: air raid sirens sounded to warn of bombing raids.

The whole operation was constructed in great screcy, but on the day the site became operational a propaganda broadcast from Germany by 'Lord Haw Haw' announced to the British People:

Germany calling…Germany calling…Watnall, we know your secret…' The broadcast continued to give details of the location of the bunker and its operation. RAF Group 12 H.Q. had been rumbled: *Watnall had a spy!*

Propaganda Broadcasts were made daily by William Joyce. Jokingly called 'Lord Haw Haw,' from the Abwehr Radio Station in Hamburg. It was illegal to tune in, but nine million of us did. The news was often up –to-date and accurate: 'This morning the clock on Darlington Town Hall is two minutes slow!' Haw Haw also announced the resignation of our War Minister: Hore Belisha, before the BBC broadcast the story, this unnerved the government. Haw Haw was no longer a joke.

Official line was *'There are no German Spies in Britain,' they have all been intercepted.* This was far from true. Secret information about places like Watnall was relayed to Germany in Morse Code from Transmitters hidden in attics and brief cases.
Lord Haw Haw was executed for treason in 1946.
The Watnall Spy was never found.

Roger continues: After WW11 we ran headlong into 'The Cold War' and in the 1950's the Watnall Bunker structure was 'hardened'to withstand a nuclear attack. I have the original plans. It became part of the 'Home Chain' network, receiving signals from the East Coast chain of Radar Stations, giving early warning of a Soviet Attack. Watnall then relayed the signals to USAF Mildenhall and Lakenheath where nuclear armed Bombers were on standbye. These would be on their way to Moscow before the Soviet bombers put us out of action. It all relied on rapid signal analysis and quick action to get the US bombers airborne.

In charge of the control room that morning was a young RAF operator, John, who later became a doctor and emigrated to New Zealand. John sent me a hair-raising letter about how close we came to armageddon on Christmas day in 1953 , when by some split-second thinking and quick phone calls , we managed to get fighter planes off the ground and were able to report to USAF ATC that signals of a Soviet attack was a false alarm caused by freak weather conditions.

'Friends of Brinsley Headstocks'

The Friends of Brinsley Headstocks was formed in 2008. We work in close partner-shipwith the site's owners, Broxtowe Borough Council. The objectives of the group are:

* To develop the site's wildlife potential.
* To develop and preserve the last remaining timber-tandem
  headstocks in the country.
* To protect and promote the site's mining and literary heritage.
* To develop the site as an educational resource.
* To raise funds for the site and to enable the group to carry on its
  work.

The heritage and nature reserve is on the site of the former Brinsley

Colliery, which was in production in 1842. The tandem headstocks which we see today were obtained second-hand from nearby Willey Lane colliery and were erected in Brinsley in 1872. The pit was closed in 1930 and was eventually abandoned in 1934, although the shafts were kept open until 1970 to provide access and ventilation to Moorgreen and Pye Hill pits. In 1970 the surface buildings were demolished and the headstocks were donated to Lound Hall Mining Museum, near Retford. When the museum closed in 1989, the headstocks were returned to Brinsley and were erected close to their original location, although they were approximately two metres shorter, due to being cut free from the concrete foundations at Lound Hall.

The cultural significance of the site stems from the fact that D.H. Lawrence's father and his father's three brothers all worked at Brinsley Colliery. One of Lawrence's uncles, James, lived in Vine cottage, which is the derelict building adjacent to the headstocks car park. James lived in the cottage with his wife Polly and their two children, but he was killed by a roof fall at Brinsley pit, just a month before Polly gave birth to a daughter. D. H. Lawrence recorded this disaster in his play "The Widowing of Mrs. Holroyd" and the main character of his short story "The Odour of Chrysanthemums" was based on his Aunt Polly.

The Friends of Brinsley Headstocks are also responsible for preserving and developing the wildlife habitat on the site. We were proud to be awarded **Local Nature Reserve status in 2008** and were equally delighted when part of the site was designated a **Site of Interest For Nature Conservation (SINC) in 2010.** Since taking over responsibility of the site, we have improved habitat and biodiversity considerably, not least by the creation of five wildlife ponds, where previously there were none. Our current conservation efforts are habitat creation specifically for hedgehogs (which have declined by an alarming 96.6% in the last 70 years) and Willow Tit (which has declined by 91% since 1967). We have regular working parties where our members get their hands dirty; digging, planting, sowing wildflower seed, litter-picking etc. New members are always welcome, with no restrictions on age, ability or place of residence.

The Headstocks Festival is held every year in early September, which in addition to the numerous stalls and activities, includes guided walks around the site, explaining it's historical and wildlife importance.

John Eyre.

Widlife Recorder, Friend of Brisley Headstocks.

Brinsley Headstocks Nature Reserve

BRINSLEY ANIMAL RESCUE

NOTTINGHAM

REGISTERED CHARITY 1135508

brinsleyanimalrescue.org

Heanor, Derbyshire.

(Courtesy of Heanor and District Local History Society)

This hilltop market town is the birthplace of acclaimed nineteenth century writer William Howitt. William wrote and published dozens of books and younger brother Richard was a distinguished poet. Known amongst others for 'The Gypsy King.' William and his wife Mary founded the Howitt Primary School,

Harry Riley's note: the following story of the supernatural, concerns this eminent Heanor family and is reprinted here with the kind permission of the **Heanor and District Local History Society:**

The most famous ghost story of the area, dating from 1795, is told by William Howitt to the author R.D. Owen in his book: 'Footfalls on the Boundary of Another World.'[1860]

"One fine afternoon, my mother [Phoebe Howitt], shortly after a confinement, but perfectly convalescent, was lying in bed enjoying from her window the sense of summer beauty and repose, a bright sky above and the quiet village before her. In this state she was gladdened by hearing the footsteps which she took to be those of her brother Frank [Francis Tantum], as he was familiarly called, approaching the door. The visitor knocked and entered. The foot of the bed was towards the door, and the curtains at the foot, notwithstanding the season, were drawn to prevent the draught. Her brother parted them and looked in upon her. His gaze was ernest and destitute of its usual cheerfulness and he spoke not a word. 'My dear Frank' said my mother,. 'How glad I am to see you! Come round to the bedside; I wish to have some talk with you.'

He closed the curtains, as complying, but instead of doing so, my mother to her astonishment, heard him leave the room, close the door behind him, and begin to descend the stairs. Greatly amazed, she hastily rang, and when her maid appeared she bade her call her brother back. The girl replied that she had not seen him enter the house. But my mother insisted, saying 'He was here but this instant. Run! Quick! Call him back! I must see him!'

The girl hurried away, but after a time returned, saying that she could learn nothing of him anywhere; nor had anyone in or about the house seen him either enter or depart. Now my father's house stood at the bottom of the village and close to the high road, which was quite straight; so that anyone passing along it must have been seen for a much longer period than had elapsed. The girl said she had looked up and down the road, then searched the garden-a large old-fashioned one, with shady walks. But neither in the garden, nor on the road was he to be seen. She had enquired at the nearest cottages in the village, but no one had seen him pass.

"My mother, though a very pious woman, was far from superstitious; yet the strangeness of this circumstance struck her forcibly.

While she lay pondering upon it, there was heard a sudden rushing and excited talking in the village street.

My mother listened: it increased, though up to that time the village had been profoundly still; and she became convinced that something very unusual had occurred. Again she rang the bell, to enquire the cause of the disturbance. This time it was the monthly nurse who answered it. She sought to tranquillize my mother, as a nurse usually does to a patient:' Oh, it is nothing particular, ma'am,' she said 'Some trifling affair!', which she pretended to relate, passing lightly over the particulars. But her ill-suppressed agitation did not escape my mother's eye. 'Tell me the truth.' She said, 'at once! I am certain something very sad has happened.' The woman still equivocated, fearing the effect upon my mother in her situation. And at first the family joined in the attempt at concealment. Finally however, my mother's entreaties drew from them the terrible truth that her brother had been stabbed at the top of the village and killed on the spot.

''The melancholy event had thus occurred: My uncle, Francis Tantum, had been dining at Shipley Hall, with Mr. Edward Miller Mundy, member of Parliament for the county.

Shiply Hall lay off to the left of the village as you looked on the main street from my father's house, and about a mile distant from it; while Heanor Fall, my uncle's residence, was situated to the right;

the road to the one country seat and to the other, crossing, nearly at right angles, the upper portion of the village street at a point where stood one of the two village inns, the 'Admiral Rodney' [later renamed the Old Crown Inn], respectably kept by the widow H-ks [Hanks]. I remember her well - a tall, fine looking woman, who must have been handsome in her youth, and who retained, even past middle age, an air superior to her condition. She had only one child, a son, then scarcely twenty. He was a good looking, brisk young fellow, and bore a very fair character. He must, however, as the event showed, have been of a very hasty temper.

"Francis Tantum, riding home from Shipley Hall after the early country dinner of that day, somewhat elate it may be with wine, stopped at the widow's inn and bade her son bring him a glass of ale. As the latter hurried to obey, my uncle, giving the youth a smart switch across the back with his riding-whip, cried out in his lively, joking way, **'Now be quick, Dick; be quick!'**

"The young man, instead of receiving the playful stroke as a jest, took it as an insult. He rushed into the house, snatched up a carving knife, and darting into the street, stabbed my uncle to the heart as he sat on his horse, so that he fell dead on the instant, in the road.

"The sensation throughout the quiet village may be imagined. The inhabitants who idolized the murdered man, were prevented from taking summary vengeance on the homicide only by the constables carrying him off to the office of the nearest magistrate. Young H-ks was tried at the next Derby Assizes; but [justly, no doubt, taking into view the sudden irritation caused by the blow] he was convicted of manslaughter only, and, after a few months imprisonment, returned to the village, where. Notwithstanding the strong popular feeling against him, he continued to keep the inn, even after his mother's death. He is still present, to my recollection, a quiet, retiring man, never guilty of any other irregularity of conduct, and seeming to bear about with him the constant memory of his rash deed- a silent blight upon his life.

"So great was the respect entertained for my uncle, and such the deep impression of his tragic end, that so long as that generation lived, the church bells of the village were regularly tolled on the anniversary of his death. "On comparing the circumstances and the exact time at which each occurred, the fact was substantiated that the apparition presented itself to my mother almost immediately after her brother had received the fatal stroke."

Heanor & District Local History Society

Heanor and District Local History Society has a thriving membership, publishing many books and information / historical fact sheets of Heanor then and now. Their monthly meetings are often packed to capacity with regular talks given by well known local history buffs such as Brian Key and Robert Mee, (Treasurer and Webmaster.)

Just like nearby neighbour-Eastwood, Heanor town prospered by its rich coal mining heritage, Textile manufacturing, the railways and the Erewash and Nottingham canals.

The Howitt's were one of several prominent families of Heanor, and William and his wife Mary founded a community school, which still survives and thrives at Heanor to this day. Wm. was a prolific writer and here is a short extract from one of his many books which really brings to life the reality of those grim, early days of local coal mining for men, women and young boys:

Wm. Howitt's Boys Country Book of 1839

(He relates through the eyes of a wealthy young boy as he rides his pony towards the coal pits owned by his father)…

"I first saw the coal-pits by night. As I rode over a hill, I suddenly perceived before me in every direction, strange lights, that only seemed to make the darkness deeper. Melancholy sounds, as of groans and sighings, and wild lamentings, came upon my ear, and fell awfully upon my heart. I could perceive by the fires that blazed here and there in a hundred places, that a wild landscape was before me; and Burman, the man I accompanied

-

(my father's clerk) told me it was full of coal-pits; that these fires were burning by them; and that the sounds I heard were the sounds of the machinery by which the coal was drawn up, and of the steam-engines by which the pits were cleared of water. As we went on we soon approached one of the coal pits, and a wild scene it was. In two or three tall cressets (metal baskets) fires were flaming and flickering in the wind; on the ground other large fires were burning, and by their light I could see black figures standing or moving about.

Around were other paler fires, that with a smothered force seemed burning dimly, and every now and then breaking up with a stream of flame, and then dying away again. The flames gleamed ruddily on the colliers: on their great wailing wheels and tall timbers; and on the immence stacks of coals that stood around. It required daylight and further aquaintance with the place and people to dispel my awe. When these came, and I had looked about me, I discovered many objects of interest. I found that the smothered fires that I had seen were coke fires; that is, fires in which they burn soft coal to coke or mineral charcoal, in the same way that in the forests they burn wood into charcoal by piling it up in heaps, covering it up from the air, and letting it burn without flames by which it is made useful for burning in chafing dishes(Braziers) for the purpose of many kinds of mechanics and for the drying kilns of millers, maltsters etc.

I found the pits, awful gulphs (circular holes) of some yards wide, and an immense depth: some sixty or seventy yards deep. Others as much as two hundred yards deep. A terrible place one of these pits seemed to me, far more than those old forsaken ones where I had gone to seek birds nests, because they were half concealed by bushes; and these standing wide open to the day. I shuddered to see the colliers go near them, much more to see them seat themselves on a single chain, hook it to the end of the huge rope that hung over this terrible chasm, and suffer themselves to be thus let down to the bottom.

These pits were very old fashioned pits. They were not worked by steam engines, which in those days merely drew water, but by which the coals are now whirled up, and the men are whirled down with a fearful speed. They were worked only by a huge wheel, with one end of its axle on the earth and the other fixed to the beam above. This wheel, which they called a Gin wheel, was turned round by a couple of horses; and a large rope uncoiling one way as it coiled the other round the gin, drew up the coal, and let down the chain for more at the same time. At the mouth of the pit a man stood with an iron hook, and as the coal came up piled on a sledge called a cauf and secured by wooden frames called garlands, he seized the ring in the end of the cauf and drew the coal to land. At one of these pits a girl once performed this office and missing her foot as she approached the pit mouth to hook the load of coal, plunged headlong into the pit and was dashed to pieces. But what was the most sad of all was, that the person who was first at the bottom to hear her fall , and who came and found the mangled corpse, was her own father.

On every pit-hill as they call it, that is, on the mound that surmounts the pit made by the earth thrown out in digging it, the colliers have a cabin, often built of coal. In this they keep a good fire in cold weather, and here when they have done their work they often sit and drink ale and make merry. A rude and uncouth crew they look; yet I found them a very honest, good-natured set of fellows; and I delighted to sit on a great coal with them, and hear them tell their country stories, of which they have abundance, and "many a random shot of country wit." One very odd custom they have, and that is giving a nickname to every workman: and what is odder still, this is said to be the custom in every part of the country where there are colliers. You might live amongst them for months before you get to hear their real names. You would hear them calling one another only by such names as these: Stump, Swimp, Drummer, Old Soul, Moon-eye, Gentleman Tom, Bogard Tom (Bogard is a ghost), Old Strokes, Two Powers, Kettle-bender and Crack-a-marble.

These were names all known to me; and what is as singular, everybody and everything was called old: mere lads, dogs, cats, horses, or anything that they spoke of familiarly were old. It was not expressive of age but of good fellowship.

Many a day did I use to spend amongst these black and honest mortals. I used to climb upon their stacks of coals, that extended far and wide, a sable wilderness, and there I found many a treasure of a wagtail nest. At length I mustered courage to go down a pit - yes, down one of those dreadful gulphs of which no bottom could be seen, but up which came a thin blue vapour, and a sound of falling waters. Oh! It was a terrible moment when we were swung off, over the pit mouth and it made me sick and giddy. The rope appeared to dwindle to a hair, and below I dared not look, but I thought to what a horrible, unknown depth I was going! Down, however, we went. Around us gushed water from the bricks which lined the side of the pit, and fell with a dreary, splashing sound, far, far below.

I looked up-the daylight appeared only a small, circular, intense speck, like a star above me; and presently I heard below human voices sounding deeply like echoes. To my vast delight we soon felt the solid ground beneath us. A collier unhooked my protector from his chain and we stood at the entrance of a region of darkness."

Harry Riley's note...

I hope this incredibly vivid account of those early mines has given our readers an appetite to read more of this: Wm. Howitt's Boys Country Book of 1839; just as it has for me.

Local Sporting Stars

Jeff Astle: By his brother Ken and wife Marion Astle

Jeff was born on 13th May 1942 on Nottingham Road Eastwood. He was the youngest of four brothers: Jim: Garry: Ken: Jeff and sister Lilian. The family moved to Greenhills Road, Eastwood, where they were brought up. Tragedy struck the family in 1945 when Dad (Samuel) died and Mum had to go out to work to support us, no benefits in those days.

Most of our time as youngsters was spent playing football on Mansfield Road Recreation Ground with other friends from Greenhill's Road. On Sundays the brothers attended Brinsley Churches as choirboys. Mum used to give them one penny each for their bus fares but they used to spend it at the local shop on sweets, hoping someone would spot them walking and stop and give them a lift to church.

Mum remarried to new Dad: Harry Coakley who took us under his wing and they had two children: Margaret and Susan. One of the highlights Mablethorpe, armed with tents and gradually progressing to caravans and boarding houses. They used to spend every day playing football and cricket on the beach, swimming in the sea in their homemade for swimming trunks which consisted of an old woollen jumper with the neck sewn up and the sleeves cut out to fit their legs through, all held up with a 'snake belt'. Imagine the sight when they came out of the the Astle children was their annual fortnight's holiday to sea,wet woollen jumper sagging at their knees, what a sight!

Another favourite haunt was Jacksons Arcade where Jeff and Garry used to spend their few pennies on the slot machines whilst brother Ken spent his money on ice creams and prawns, taunting them, when both were skint.

Jeff attended Devonshire Drive School and at the age of ten he became captain of the schools junior football team mentored by Mr. Morley, the school's sports teacher. He was selected to play for West Notts junior and later the senior boys teams. He then attended Walker Street school and was outstanding in his football abilities, especially at heading a ball. He was soon playing in the senior side at the age of 11.

Jeff also loved playing cricket with his brothers, he was an outstanding player and could easily have taken this sport up professionally. They played for Eastwood United and later for many years at Eastwood Town Cricket Club winning many trophies and medals.

On leaving school Jeff got a job as an apprentice fitter at Moorgreen Colliery but after a short while decided it was not the career he wanted to pursue and left. He then signed amateur forms for Notts County on the groundstaff but shortly after signing, Notts had to cut back on staff so Jeff left and found a job with John Player in Nottingham where he soon started to play football for the works team. Brothers Jim and Ken used to cycle to the John Player ground at Aspley every Saturday afternoon to watch Jeff play, (Ken's bike had been fished out of Moorgreen Reservoir by brother Gary, no posh bikes for them).

In the meantime Tommy Lawton had been replaced by Frank Hill at Notts County who summoned Jeff to his office and offered him a professional contract at the age of 17, which he immediately signed. Jeff continued. Jeff continued to play for Notts County until 1963 scoring many goals for them with his great heading ability. It was this year in December that Jeff married Laraine and they later had daughters Dorice: Dawn and Claire. He also put in a transfer request which was accepted by County.

It wasn't long before West Bromwich Albion showed an interest in Jeff and manager Jimmy Hagan and Chairman Jim Gaunt agreed terms of £25,000 for Jeff's transfer becoming an Albion player on 30th September and he played for Albion that night against Leicester City. The Albion fans took to Jeff immediately and he was soon known as "The King of the Hawthorns," they absolutely idolised him and still do to this day. He always gave his time to the fans, chatting and signing autographs whenever requested. He loved them and they loved him.

One of the most proud and memorable times for the family was when all Jeff's brothers and sisters and their families piled into a minibus (a large one) when he played in the 1968 Cup Final angainst Everton, sitting in the front row of the stands at Wembley Stadium and Jeff scoring the only goal to win the final for Albion, not much sitting when that shot went in, we were all ecstatic, although we shoudn't have been surprised as jeff had scored in every round of the F.A. Cup competition. He also played for England five times whilst at Albion. Jeff had ten glorious years playing for Albion and was given a testimonial match in October 1974 when his friend George Best played in his line up.

On leaving Albion he went on to play for Dunstble Town, Weymouth and Atherstone.

After his footballing Career ended Jeff set up his own industrial cleaning business and also through his love of singing he teamed up with Frank Skinner and David Baddiel on their TV show 'Fantasy Football' where jeff would close the show with a song. He met many famous celebrities on the show. He also started his own road shows touring the country. One of his passions, through his love of horse racing, was to attend the Cheltenham Festival, meeting up with friends Terry Biddlecomb, Josh Gifford and Billy Beaumont.

On Saturday 19th January 2002 Jeff died suddenly at his daughter Dawn's home aged 59. He died a hero to his beloved Albion fans which reflected in the vast turnout for his funeral, lining the streets of Netherseal and West Bromwich.

Following his death a Set of Gates were erected in his memory on 11th July at the Birmingham Road end of the Hawthorns Ground. He also had a Midland Metro Tram with the logo of the number nine emblazoned on it. More recently when the Eastwood Comprehensive School changed its status to Hall Park Academy one of the School houses was named 'Astle House' in memory of famous people from Eastwood.

The coroners report on Jeff's death stated he died of a degenerative brain disease caused by excessive heading of the football. 'The **Justice for Jeff Campaign'** was launched by Jeff's family, calling for an independent inquiry regarding this verdict. The West Brom fans made a point of applauding for one minute on the nineth minute of every home game in tribute to Jeff.

It was announced on 26th March 2015 the club would be holding 'Astle Day' in memory of Jeff on 11th April at the Hawthornes. The ground was packed to the rafters with all his adoring fans and also marked the beginning of **'The Jeff Astle Foundation'** which his wife Laraine and his daughters had tirelessly worked to bring about.

Harry Riley's note: What a fantastic story of local boy makes good. To my mind this is vintage boy's-own stuff-magical inspiration for every youngster to read. Straight out of the pages of Roy of the Rovers! I can certainly echo those comments about the tribute game for Jeff-the King, being filled to the rafters as I had the great fortune to be present at the match sitting alongside my pal and co-researcher: Brian Fretwell and Ken Woodhead (Mayor of Eastwood) Our story of this extraordinary day is recorded in Volume one: Eastwood Nottinghamshire Times Past and Present. Our Mayor, wearing his official chain of office, was interviewed on the giant television screen above and inside the Hawthornes ground and he was mobbed by young football fans demanding his autograph.

Having lived and worked in Eastwood all his life, Brian Fretwell reflects on his sporting pals including Jeff Astle…

'Jeff was one of four well known footballers from the Eastwood area, Tony Woodcock made his name with Notts Forest and England before moving on to Germany. Alan and Steve Buckley were coached from a very early age by their Dad - Tom. Playing for Notts and Derby in turn, Alan later taking up managementat Grimsby Town. I think Eastwood should become part of this foundation in honour of Jeff's skills and entertainment, he bought to football supporters in the town.

During the 1990's I would meet up with Jeff at Uttoxeter Races.
'These were meetings he very rarely missed. He never altered in the fifty years I have known him. He always asked about Eastwood and certain people in the community, and he married a local girl: Laraine. His football ability took him to the top of the ladder, playing for England after moving to a bigger club in W.B.A.'
On Saturday April 11th 2015 Jeff was honoured by West Brom at the Hawthorns ground with 'Astle Day' at the W.B.A. v Leicester City match, the home team wearing a replica of their 1968 Cup Final kit- plain white shirts and shorts and red socks. The sad thing being that Jeff had passed away not remembering anything about that glorious moment when he'd scored the winning goal, the day when he'd felt so proud that 'he could jump over the stands,' the day when he'd become 'The King' and and a legend to all those fans.
It all began in 1942, Jeff was born in a Co-Op house on Nottingham Road Eastwood, opposite S. Perry's confectioners shop. He was the youngest of five children and attended Devonshire Drive School aged 5 until he was 11.

The headmaster: Mr. Sprittlehouse, an avid football supporter and a Notts County Scout, spotted exceptional talent in Jeff's ability, getting him on the ground staff at an early age.

Devonshire Drive School Football Team 1952–53
Mr Morley,John Clarke,Mick Kirby,Terry Dring,Roy
Grainger,Barry Hickling,Tony Wardle,Tony Bevan,Mr
Sprittlehouse
Front Row.
Vic Allen,Jeff Astle,Arthur Rowley,Peter George,Terry
Whelan

Jeff Astle heading ball   Eastwood Town Cricket Club : Jeff scond left
                                              Bottom row

In those days Jeff's transport for training at Meadow Lane Mon-Friday was by bus and fellow footballers would travel back with him. Local lads from 'The Buildings' and the Eastwood area met up on Sunday Afternoons on Mansfield Road Recreation ground. For a knock-about from 2pm onwards after most of them had topped up with 'Shippo's Ale' to deaden the pain of a misplaced kick on the shins. Any sort of boots were worn-Pit boots, Farm boots, Wellington boots etc.etc. Many a time, a boot would fly through the air during a game.'

'Unfortunately Jeff was not allowed to play in these knock-abouts though, owing to his commitments to Notts County.'

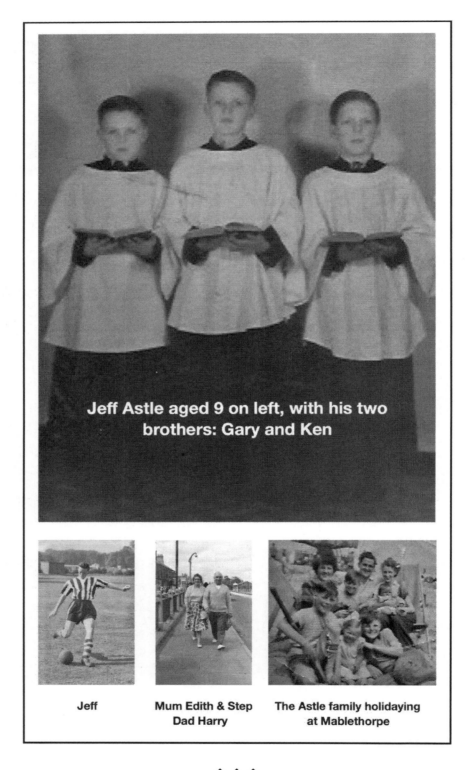

Jeff Astle aged 9 on left, with his two brothers: Gary and Ken

Jeff

Mum Edith & Step Dad Harry

The Astle family holidaying at Mablethorpe

'The Young Jeff Astle'

By his pal: Stuart Mayes

I look back to my childhood and realise from the moment I first set eyes on Jeff it was a young life that was always going to be competitive. I had my first cricket bat and going to have a game on Eastwood's Mansfield Road Recreation Ground, it was Jeff who always carried the bat and me-the ball. We both attended Devonshire Drive School where Jeff became a player in a successful school team, becoming a prolific goal scorer. At 11 years old and now at Walker Street School, Jeff started to develop at both football and cricket. Looking back on those early years I remember occasions like the time we had a pair of 'stilts' each and it wasn't long before we were in the shelter on the recreation ground and playing football on stilts. During the mid 1950's Jeff's elder brother: Jim and a group of older cricketers re-formed Eastwood Cricket Club and all the Astle family re-built the now derelect pavilion on 'The Breach'. The next 5 years saw Jeff develop as a very accomplished all-rounder.

1957 saw Eastwood Town C.C. playing on The Breach. Jeff at 15 years old was playing as a medium-pace bowler and number 3 batsman. It was two years later that players like Arthur Rowley, Albert Wardle, Bernard Gill, Sid Beresford, Alan White, Gordon Smithurst, and Ken Aldred, to name but a few, joined the club. Jeff developed into a high scoring batsman and a very accurate pace bowler.

During our early teens we both had a bike, this turned as usual into a competition. We would race to Underwood and back. Jeff always went through Brinsley and back down to Moorgreen. I would go the opposite way. Jeff would always win because he did not have to climb Hunt's Hill. The only time I beat him was when I held onto a tractor and trailer going up Hunt's Hill.

When Jeff joined Notts County Football Club he took up snooker and it wasn't long before he became good at it, which was no surprise, this led to nights spent in the club at the top of Alexander Street and it was always Jeff coming out on top. My dad was a very useful Billiards and Snooker player, so we used to go to a Billiard Hall in Ilkeston on Sunday mornings and I became a better player and able to give Jeff a more competitive game.

Going back to Jeff's early football career he would play for Notts County on Saturday but would always turn out on Mansfield Road Recreation Ground on a Sunday afternoon. These games to Jeff were just as competitive as a Saturday. At this time Jeff started to work on his game and we would work on long passes. I would turn up on the right wing and he would hit the balls to me with his left foot, then I would turn around and he would hit the balls with his right foot. The session would end with canes in a line and we would take it in turns to dribble around the canes, going out with the right foot and back with the left. As usual this was against the clock and we didn't go back until he had won more than me.

Jeff will always be remembered as a lad who never said a wrong word about anyone and who always had a smile on his face.

RIP Jeff...Stuart Mayes

1953 at The Palmerston Arms: Left to Right: R. Rayworth: T. Severn: R. George: M. Brown: S. Mayes: J. Astle: B.Severn: K. Astle: P. George.

Jeff Astle: Barry Severn: Stuart Mayes 'at Jeff's 50th Birthday'

Jeff Astle, third boy from left on the back row, pictured during his Walker Street, Eastwood schooldays. Mr. Allen is the teacher on the left of the picture.

Basford Bystander

Basford & District Community Newspaper

Covering Old and New Basford, Aspley, Cinderhill, Hyson Green, Carrington, Radford, Broxtowe, Highbury Vale etc

June/July 2016 Every Other Month 35p

Stan Smith   1937 - 2016

Contents

Tribute to Stan Smith
Memories of Leonard Street
Hyson Green Youth Club - Early Days
Mill Street, Old Basford
Local Pubs
High Pavement Trip - Feedback

Issue

176

Plus regular feature:
Monthly Diary with meetings of clubs, societies, churches and local organisations.

he could devote as much time as he wanted to writing, and spent many hours on the computer and internet researching his work.

Stan joined the Basford & District Local History Society shortly after its inception in 1984. The then Secretary, Brenda Summers, and four other members of the Society formed a Community Newspaper which they called "Basford Bystander", the idea of which was to record people's memories and publicise local clubs and

Stan Smith in the garden   Brinsley Church Re-opening

Stan Smith Eulogy By Christine Smith

"**Stan had always wanted to write** and during his working life got up early to work on the typewriter – this in the time before home computers. After retirement he could devote as much time as he wanted to writing, and spent many hours on the computer and Internet researching his work. Stan joined the Basford & district Local History Society after its inception in 1984. The then Secretary: Brenda Summers and four members of the society forned a Community Newspaper which they called 'The

Basford Bystander' the idea of which was to record people's memories and publicise local clubs and events. Brenda acted as the editor.

Stan became involved as he was interested in the history of the Basford area, much of Old Basford having been lost to demolition in the 1960s. He did a lot of research and wrote many articles for the Bystander.

Following the untimely death of Brenda Summers, Stan took over the editorship of the Bystander which he continued to do from 2001 until he passed away in 2016.

Stan also wrote many books about Brinsley, Underwood and surrounding villages, under the pen name of Ztan Zmith, the proceeds of which were donated to the churches in those villages. This was particularly helpful towards the re-ordering of Brinsley Church, which meant it could be used for community events as well as a place of worship.

He enjoyed doing research, going to interview people and writing their reminiscences. History played an important part in his life and most of his writing revolved around this. Although he also wrote short stories and poetry for the Nottingham Writers' Club monthly competitions.

Stan also gave talks to local groups about the history in his books and about writing. Never without a notebook, which was later replaced by a miniature tape recorder, anything and everything interested him.

He would always say that writing the book was the easiest part, the hard part was selling them. So all his books and display aids were regularly packed in the car and displayed on a stand at the church garden party, fete, historical event, book fair, etc.

As time passed and more people came to know his books, they would eagerly wait for the latest one to come out and Stan would organise a book launch. A website and internet also helped to spread the word.

It is hoped to keep the Basford Bystander in print for at least in the short to medium term."

Christine Smith

Carole's Snack Bar
Giltbrook

/

//////New venture by local couple Dave and Carole Harwood, Carole's Snack Bar in its beautiful new premises offers a variety of breakfast and lunch menus to either eat in or takeaway. We have a seating capacity of 30 inside and a further 10 outside. Dave was born at Oaks farm Moorgreen in 1958, he attended Underwood infants school and later Mathew Holland Comprehensive at Selston, after leaving school he worked on the farm with his father Bill Harwood and his older brother Jimmy Harwood for over 20 years. Dave then worked at Birnam Products New Eastwood for 17 years until its closure/. Dave below, as a 5 year old boy playing in the farmyard at Oaks farm.

///Carole was born in 1959 eldest daughter of Mike and Irene Hatton, she started life in Awsworth, later moving to Newthorpe were she attended Beauvale school and later Eastwood Comprehensive. After leaving school she worked at Meridian Ilkeston and Wolsey at Kimberly, which at that time was part of a thriving sewing trade. While the children were growing up she worked in school meals at Brookhill Leys primary school Eastwood. In 1994 she started working at Birnams Products and stayed there for 17 years until its closure. When both were made redundant in October 2011 they started a small catering business. Carole's Snack Bar stood outside 'Screwfix' Giltbrook for 4 years, until January 2017 when the business moved just round the corner into a much larger premises the old Giltbrook Sound Studio.

Langley Mill and Aldercar

In volume two of our Eastwood Times Past and Present we featured the tremendous work and achievements made by volunteers of the ECP&DA, (Erewash Canal Preservation and Development Association.)

The chair of Cromford Canal Friends: John Baylis B.E.M. greatly assisted our research into the superb transformation and restoration of the Langley Mill Basin, and, as we wished to include more of the history of L/Mill in this 3rd volume he has kindly supplied a copy of a book printed to mark the Celebrations of the Coronation of King George the Fifth on Thursday June 22nd. 1911.

The souvenir hand-book was printed by local commercial printer Walter Barker, with introduction by the printer and each page having a decorative ornamental border.

This innovative printing company has now sadly gone from Langley Mill, but in the 1980's they had the distinction of being the first company to purchase a Japanese Shinahara Fuji offset lithographic colour printing press, not only in the Notts and Derby region, but in the whole of the UK, supplied by international printing machinery specialists: Graphic Arts Equipment of London (a plum order for a local saleman, yours truly-H. Riley).

The author of this potted history is William Smith Esquire, J.P. and with apologies, we reproduce his book here, minus the elaborately printed page borders and decorative woodcut fruitbowl and grapevine trimmings, reminiscent of Grinling Gibbons.

Harry Riley's note, At the ripe old age of forty I had taken the rash step of leaving the safe factory environment of commercial printing management, for the excitement and insecurity of selling international printing presses and print finishing systems to companies in the UK and abroad. This was to take me on a whirlwind career change over the next three decades, selling to newspaper and print company directors and chief executives around Europe, and the UK of course. Walter Barker Printers at Langley Mill, practically on my own doorstep, was to become the first of many printing machinery sales, and a name I will always be grateful for, even though they no longer exist.

THE CORONATION OF KING GEORGE THE FIFTH.

THURSDAY, JUNE 22nd, 1911.

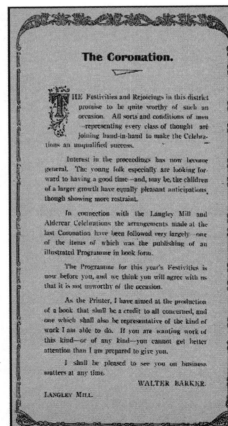

The Coronation.

THE Festivities and Rejoicings in this district promise to be quite worthy of such an occasion. All sorts and conditions of men—representing every class of thought—are joining hand-in-hand to make the Celebrations an unqualified success.

Interest in the proceedings has now become general. The young folk especially are looking forward to having a good time—and, may be, the children of a larger growth have equally pleasant anticipations, though showing more restraint.

In connection with the Langley Mill and Aldercar Celebrations the arrangements made at the last Coronation have been followed very largely—one of the items of which was the publishing of an illustrated Programme in book form.

The Programme for this year's Festivities is now before you, and we think you will agree with us that it is not unworthy of the occasion.

As the Printer, I have aimed at the production of a book that shall be a credit to all concerned, and one which shall also be representative of the kind of work I am able to do. If you are wanting work of this kind—or of any kind—you cannot get better attention than I am prepared to give you.

I shall be pleased to see you on business matters at any time.

WALTER BARKER.

LANGLEY MILL.

WILLIAM SMITH, Esq., J.P.
President of the Committee.
(Gell Badge)

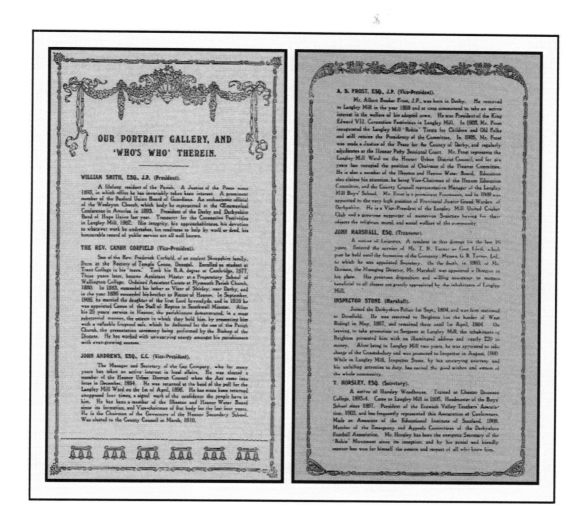

A Short History of Langley Mill

By

William Smith Esq., J.P.

Having been honoured by a request from the Coronation Committee to write a short history of Langley Mill, and as I have no ancient records to refer to, I am dependent on memory and such information as I can gather from others.

The place is principally of modern growth, and no doubt owes its name to the old water corn-mill, now dismantled and in ruins. There were indications that a water mill had been in existence at the bottom of the field where Milnhay House stands.

Langley Mill lies on the outskirts of two parishes and in two counties, the dividing line being the stream of the Erewash-except for a short distance in the middle of the place, where the course of the river seems to have been diverted.

My recollection carries me back to a period a little antecedent to the middle of the last century. I will try to depict this place as I first knew it, in comparison with the present. The main business on the Eastwood side was that connected with the canals, that on the Heanor side with a number of small collieries which were then in existence. The main portion of the people lived on the Eastwood side. Since then the centre of gravity has entirely shifted to the Heanor side. The Eastwood portion has altered considerably in the great decline of the canal business on the one hand, and the coming of the Great Northern Railway and the station they have made there, on the other, but the population is very little greater.

There were great coal wharves on the Eastwood side of the Nottingham Canal to which coals were brought from Barber, Walker and Co's, Brinsley pits on horse-tram trains-the rails being of the angle shape. There were three horses in a team and they brought in about six trams with somewhat less coal than now goes into one modern railway wagon. My father told me that he remembered teams of oxen bringing coals down from Squire Fenton's Brinsley Collieries, from New Brinsley Way. The tramway came across the fields and emerged into Langley Mill from behind the house of 'the Ganger' as the canal agent was called, and found its way upon the East side of the canal, back of 'The Great Northern Inn' across the road to a long wharf, which reached down to the next canal bridge, where old Caleb Slater's rope-walk was situated. From the trams the coal was tranferred to the boats which carried it to Nottingham, Grantham, and other places, South East. The boats which received it there carried it to Loughborough, Leicester and many other places south, and on to London.

Besides the coal carrying from Langley Mill, there was also some amount of through traffic to Cromford in Derbyshire, where was the terminus of the Cromford Canal. Wheatcroft's fly-boats came carrying general cargoes of merchandise, an important part consisting of provisions: flour, grain, etc.

Boats also discharged goods of all kinds into a warehouse-now turned into dwellings-which abutted upon the Cromford Canal, which was kept by an old gentleman who always described himself as James Brierly, Wharfinger.

A coal wharf existed on the Cromford Canal, between the canal lock and the wharehouse. I believe the coals were brought from Cresswell pit, and perhaps from the other places, for some of it came in trams, and I am informed that the coal from Cresswell's pit-which was close to the Baptist Chapel-was carted.

Another prominent feature was the lime burning which was carried on. There was a set of kilns lying between the Nottingham and Erewash canals which was carried on by a man named George Wharton, who had a farm at Old Brinsley, and another set on the west side of the Erewash Canal in the angle formed by the branch which led to the canal terminus, in the middle of the place, and coming right up to the county boundaries. The old cavities still exist. These were carried on by an old gentleman named Fletcher, who lived where Mr. Wardle now lives. 'Father' Fletcher could be seen at work on his kilns most days, either packing the stone for burning, or helping to load the 'made' lime into the farmers carts and wagons, by means of which it was principally carried away. Lime seemed in those days to play a very important part in the system of farming, and I believe also some of it was used for building purposes. The limestone was brought down the Cromford Canal from Bull Bridge.

There was at one time a Windmill which stood in the middle of Langley Mill, somewhere just about the canal terminus, but all the Eastwood side of Langley Mill was devoted to coal wharves and general canal business, and a floating population of boatmen and their wives and families was constantly in evidence.

By way of indicating the change of ideas about dwellings, I would point out there are some old cottages in the yard behind the Great Northern Inn which were then about the best style of workmen's dwellings. I have referred to The Great Northern Inn. It was then called 'The Junction Navigation' but was very often called 'the Jawbone'-from having the jawbone of a whale fixed up against the door, brought no doubt, on the canal from Hull.

Coming to the industrial life of the Derbyshire side, the coal wharf was still in evidence as far as the canal extended. I do not doubt there may be several of our old neighbours who could have helped me on this subject, but the one whom I thought would perhaps know as much or more of coal pits than anyone else was Mr. Enoch Davis, of 35 Cromford Road. Mr. Davis's term of recollection dates no further back than mine, but he entered Langley Mill a full grown man at the time that I was a young child.

I should like to mention, as one of the oldest, perhaps the very oldest survivor of colliery workers-Mr. Isaac Wilson, who lives close to the Baptist Chapel. Mr Wilson was not a collier, but what we called an engine-wright. About sixty years ago, when employed by the Butterley Company, at repair-work in a pumping shaft, in a pit somewhere near Dunstead , he had a fall of 18 yards and was brought home to die, and people enquired: 'is he dead yet?' His amazing constitution carried him through and he still lives, now in his ninetieth year.

Mr. Davis's experience was similar to that of many old colliers. He was born at Shipley Wood and commenced life as a collier boy at the age of eight and a half years. In those days, the men and boys were let down hanging in chains and holding on to the rope with their hands. There were about 6 or 8 men and boys in a bunch. There were no guide ropes. They swung about from side to side as they went up and down. They were let down in the morning so that 'winding' could commence at six o'clock and it was often eight at night before they had finished 'the day.' They had to 'turn' so many waggons to make a day, and when Saturday came, they were often so much short of of having made five days, they had to work until Saturday afternoon to do half a day and a 'tuncheon' to complete the five days. I have many times seen these bunches of men and boys coming up out of the pits with the chain only around one leg, the pits being perhaps, 20 yards deep.

What follows about the pits around Langley Mill is largely from information supplied by Mr. Davis:

'My father and a man named Goodwin were partners in getting the coal on Milnhay farm. It was carried down to the canal and loaded in boats which came and lay in the two arms of the terminus. One of the pits, and of the sinking of which I myself was a witness, about 1850, was close to the railway, and the shaft was just about where Messrs. Lovatt's offices are, but perhaps a little further from the road. This was the only pit they had which was worked by an engine. They called it a 'whimsey', it was a small affair. There was another pit worked by an engine, close to the Baptist Chapel. I don't remember to whom that belonged. Then there was one just at the top of Bakewell's Orchard which belonged to Cresswell's. The Milnhay Colliery Co., with which my father was connected, had two pits in the field between Milnhay Road and the Midland Railway. The coals from these were raised by a 'gin', turned by a horse. I well remember being taken down one of them in the dinner interval, and sitting at one end of a tub whilst a man held a younger brother, and sat at the other end, and feeling rather uncomfortable as the tub slowly descended and swung to and fro in the shaft. The same firm also sank a pit in the field at the back of where Messrs. Turner's offices are, and I remember, when they were boring to test the coal. A man coming into my father's office with a small piece of coal in his hand and saying in a triumphant voice: 'Here it is mester, there's carn i' Egypt yet! The coals from this pit were carted to the canal.

There used to be a good bit of 'swarming' up and down the pit ropes in these shallow mines, and indeed there was not much care taken of life or limb. We all rejoice in the safeguards and precautions which exist today, but I bear my testimony to the old colliers, that they were a brave, hardy race, very alert, resourceful and full of self-help. The accidents were surprisingly few, considering the dangers they had to pass through.'

Coals came down in trams from pits at Dunstead. These chiefly belonged to the Shipley Colliery. Mr. Davis says that he himself sank eight pits in that field at Dunstead, through which the footpath runs from Dunstead Lane towards Cromford Road. They were for winding, ventilating and pumping. The number was determined by a 'fault' which divided the coal. In one of these pumping shafts his father lost his life. He stepped over the unprotected brink in the dark of an early winter morning, and was killed instantly. The shaft was thirty one yards deep. Coal was also got on the East side of Dunstead Lane, and coming further down into Langley Mill, the same man got coal on the east side of the Midland Railway in the direction where the colliery line joins the railway. On asking Mr. Davis how near these shallow coals could be worked to the surface, he said, referring to this latter region, 'I once worked so near the top, the ground fell in, and I could see daylight and crawled out to the surface between two sleepers.' This was on to the tramway from Messrs. Barber & Walker's colliery.

The tramway from Dunstead came past the South end of East View Terrace (not then in existence) through the tunnel, under the Midland Railway, across the road, and through what is now Mr. Bowes' slaughter house, being carried over the Erewash on a wooden bridge and the coals weighed at a little office, still in existence, in a somewhat dilapidated state, and so on to the wharf.

Coming to the consideration of the aspect of the place on the Derbyshire side, it was a place of fields-grass and arable, with a few cottages here and there. From the style of the building, the old part can still be discovered, and if anyone will take the trouble to walk about and in a note book, jot down the old buildings, they may see how few they were.

The only place of worship in those days was the Baptist Chapel. It was generally called 'Bakewell's Chapel', and there is an inscription upon a stone in a wall inside which reads, 'Sacred to the memory of John Bakewell who died December 12th , 1846. Aged 72. Builder and clearer of this chapel for the preaching of the Gospel according to the doctrine and discipline of the New Connexion of the General Baptists.'

There is no school building whatever. Most of the children who went to school at all, went to the National School at Eastwood.

My first recollection was of going to a school at Eastwood kept by an old spinster, down below the church. Some girls from Langley Mill-the Fletchers and Bowes' went, and small boys up to about seven years were admitted. In these days of free education, when some parents don't seem to care to send their children to school, it is well to remember that there were poor people, with the father's wages only in the 'tens' of shillings, who paid 4d. per week, per head, for their children to be taught, spending as much as 1/- per week out of their scanty income to save their children from growing up in ignorance. The boys of the same families I have mentioned, went to Mr. Roscoe's School at Heanor, a private one kept in a house close to the Parish Church.

Where Aldercar Schools now are, a farmhouse used to stand, in which the late Mr. Towson was born.

In the 'Luddite' Rebellion of 1817, the rebels from Pentrich called there, on their way to Nottingham, and because the farm man would not join them they shot him dead.

As they went on through Langley Mill, seeking to gather recruits, a Mr. Burton, agent to Messrs. Barber, Walker and Co., who lived near the swing bridge, hid himself in the pig-stye, and all who could, kept out of sight.

The most pretentious dwelling was Milnhay House, occupied by Mr. Joseph Grammer, who lived with his widowed mother. The Grammers owned the Milnhay farm, which extended over what is now the busiest and most thickly peopled portion of Langley Mill.

It lay on both sides of the Midland Railway, the station being built on land acquired by the Railway Company from the Grammers. Where Bank House and Miss Woodhouse's property now stands is part of it, and all along by the Gas Works to Messrs. Frost's foundry, and on the other side, all the land occupied by the pottery and the Vulcan Works, and with some small exceptions, including all the land up to about where the United Methodist Church stands. At the corner where Mr. Henshaw's shop is, there was a pond.

Opposite Milnhay House there was a cottage farm, owned by a family called Bunting. Besides the coal mining already referred to, a considerable quantity was mined by Mr. Gregory who, at that time, owned and occupied Godkin House and the land adjoining.

There was a great lawsuit about eighty years ago between the local landowners and the lords of the manor, Mr. Mundy of Shipley, and Mr. Charlton, of Chilwell, about the ownership of the coals, in which the local men suffered seriously, as it ended in a compromise which took away from the local men all the coal on the east side of a line drawn from Aldercar along the Milnhay Road.

In this lawsuit, old deeds were produced, showing that a certain Sir John Zouch, of Codnor Castle, leased coals in the reign of good Queen Bess, so that this is a very old mining region.

Besides coal mining, lime burning, and canal trade, there were no industries in the place. The corn mills were there, but in my first recollections they were very small affairs. One was the old, ruined water mill and the other, which had an engine, was spoken of impressively as the 'steam' mill. The latter was a comparatively recent erection, and had been built by a Mr. Joseph Bowes, who died in 1843, and whose enormous bulk was dilated upon in William Howitt's story, 'Jack of the Mill.' One of my uncles, Mr. Robert Gething, told me he was a witness of a feat of strength on the part of Joseph Bowes, seeing him carry four loads of wheat, weighing at least 56 stones, up the steps to his post-windmill at Brinsley.

The instinct of self-preservation is much more developed now, and men will not expose themselves to injury for life, by doing such foolhardy feats. I knew a boatman who, for a wager, carried eighty stones of flour, and a young relation of my own carried an eighteen stone sack of wheat twice up and down the mill stone steps, which are still in the mill yard, without touching anything to help him. It was a common feat for a man to lie down on his face, have a sack of wheat laid across his shoulders, and get up with it. And there were two families of my own relations at old Brinsley, any of the male members of which could pick up from the ground 18 stones of wheat and put it on their shoulders. The old men think there are no such men born now.

As an indication of ideas prevalent at the time I may say that Mr. Wright offered my father £50.00 towards the erection of the Wesleyan Chapel, on condition that they would provide a graveyard. If this suggestion had been carried out, in view of later developments, it would have been rather an unfortunate arrangement.

Whether the building of the Primitive Church came first, after years of endeavour to gather a congregation by services held in a chamber over Than' Hunt's stable, or whether the United Methodist Church came first, I don't know. The provision of a building of a temporary character, in Elnor Street, for Anglican worship, will be within the memory of most people, and although the years do not seem many, the congregation worshipping there, will no doubt, feel it to be an auspicious day when they take possession of the permanent structure now in the course of erection, and which will no doubt, be both spacious and beautiful. With the prospective enlargement of the Wesleyan Church, we may fairly congratulate ourselves that Langley Mill will be well provided with places for Christian worship.

In the matter of schools, I believe we have teachers who for zeal and efficiency are competent to render, and do render, most valuable service, from Mr. Thos. Horsley, headmaster of the Boy's School, downwards.

Except in the case of of the latest erection-I allude to the fine block of buildings in Sedgwick Street, we do not compare favourably with surrounding places, where schools were built by the now defunct School Boards, which did such noble work whilst in existence.

But let honour be given to whom honour is due. I believe the Butterley Company built our first block of school buildings, and the Rector of the parish a later one, and the proverb is 'you must not look a gift horse in the mouth.' Of course, the County Council, in building the last set of schools, had public money to play with, and the ratepayers had to foot the bill, and when people can ladle out of public funds they can do things handsomely. No one supposes that in educational matters we have reached finality.

In seeking to draw this short sketch to a conclusion, and in order to show the difference between the past and the present, I quote from an old Notts. Directory, which I found in my brother's library at Milnhay, dated 1853, 'Langley Bridge is about half a mile West of Eastwood, and gives name to a large village which is partly in Derbyshire. The present bridge was built in 1130 and crosses the Erewash. There are several extensive coal wharves, a steam corn mill and several lime kilns. When we come to the list of names.

I find 16 entered as in Eastwood parish and 10 in Heanor, all they say is 'Langley Mills is a village and station on the Erewash Branch of the Midland Railway, partly in this parish and partly in Eastwood. There is a large corn mill and iron foundry.' And the list of names under Langley Mills only amounts to 10, whilst under Langley there is a list of 23 names. The iron foundry was a small affair on Cromford Road, lying between the road and the railway, and was carried on by Woodward & Horsfield, and afterwards by a man named Goulder. It was at the same place where Russell, Turner & Pender fixed their works, afterwards removing to the present site of the Star Foundry, and thence the late Mr. G. R. Turner migrated to commence the works now carried on by Messrs. G. R. Turner Ltd. The Langly Mill Engineering Co., which he left, was after some years closed down until it was purchased by Messrs. Pickersgill & Frost and adapted for their business. The Pottery was started by Mr. Calvert of Belper. It was for a number of years only a small affair, until Messrs. Lovatt came and joined the first proprietor.

In their hands, it has increased until it has become one of the most prosperous concerns in the district, and is famous for its Langley Mill Art Ware to the utmost parts of the British Empire.

Summing up the present industrial condition, we may say that Langley Mill is in touch with the world. The corn mill receives its supplies of grain from Australia, South and North America, largely from our Indian Empire, and also almost constantly from the great Russian Empire, as well as from our own wheat fields. From Messrs. G. R. Turner's railway, plant is sent out to far distant lands. Messrs. Lovatt & Lovatt send their goods as far o'er the seas as Australasia, and Messrs., Frost's manufactures may be seen all over our own country. We may well consider ourselves 'quite in the swim.'

As we are on two lines of railway, Langley Mill is a place which offers great facilities for all manner of business enterprises. We have now a population gathered from many parts of England, whereas sixty years ago, or less, it was comprised almost entirely of natives.

As this sketch is written in connection with the Coronation Festivities of King George the Fifth, I will mention that when we were celebrating, in a similar manner, the Coronation of the late King Edward the Seventh, one item of our rejoicings was an 'Old Folks Tea'

At the Cooperative Society's Hall, when the late Mr. Samuel Towson Presided. In his speech after tea, he reviewed the past, and predicted a great change in the direction of improved conditions. He spoke of better food, better clothing and better homes; also of more wages and less work; more leisure; more holidays and more excursions: but the final conclusion he drew was:- 'I don't see that you are one whit happier than we were, and perhaps unconsciously, he hit upon a great truth, since none of these things can in themselves make people happy, we may remember that the eye is not satisfied with seeing, nor the ear with hearing.

In conclusion, I am sure that I may, in the name of all my neighbours, wish King George a long, prosperous, peaceful and happy reign. We believe that our King is a man whose whole desire is so to act as to promote the welfare of the people. One feature of the reign of all the Georges has been steady friends to religious liberty, and have always given the weight of their influence in favour of that great right, liberty of conscience . When I say Georges, I of course mean, equally, the late King, who showed so tactful a consideration for all his subjects, and also his honoured mother who came before him, and bluff King William too.

As sobriety is so great an asset in our national life, and one of the most tactful things the late King Edward ever did was when he made it known that it was according to his wish that all who desired to drink his health might do so in water.

I know that I am expressing the earnest desire of every member of our Coronation Committee, whose behest, I have fulfilled to the best of my ability, when I say that their great aim is that all the festivities may be carried out in a way which will reflect credit on the people of this place.

GOD SAVE THE KING AND THE PEOPLE.

The Erewash Valley branch of the Midland Railway was not opened until 1847, an event which I just remember. In Williams, 'Midland Railway,' we learn that the traffic for some time afterwards was small, a circumstance accounted for by the fact that a canal runs parrallel with it for it's entire length.' To make the matter quite clear to all, I may say that three canals had their junction at Langley Mill: the Cromford, coming from the place of that name, near Matlock, and ending at Langley Mill; the Nottingham, going on from here to that place, and the Erewash, beginning below the lock and joining the Trent not far from Long Eaton. The policy of the Railway Companies was to get control of the canals, and so the Midland Railway got control of the one from Cromford, and the Great Northern the one to Nottingham. The original proprietors still control the Erewash Canal.

The business on the railway from Langley Mill station, was, for some little while, so small, that all the carting was done by an old man named Locksley, who kept the toll bar where the Midland Hotel now stands, and who built a stable in his garden for the one horse which was sufficient for the work.

I have been asked, 'What was done at the toll bars?'

People who used the road had to pay 4½d. per horse in harness and 1½d. in the saddle. It cost 1/1½ tolls to drive to Nottingham.

A man named Howitt–a relation to the Howitts of Heanor–was the first station master. He, many years afterwards, emigrated to Canada.

The carriages for passengers were of a rude and primitive description. The third class carriages were all open from the height of the seating to the top, and when the shutters were up there was very little light. Indeed, I myself travelled, so my parents informed me, when the third class were open trucks and had no roof on at all.

Previous to the opening of the railway, no mode of travelling existed but by carriers' carts. People in general did not travel then. They stopped at home, having no money to spend. Old Mr. Fletcher, well within my time, went to Derby Market by the carrier, and helped to push up the hills. To go to Nottingham was looked upon as quite an undertaking, easily equivalent to going to London now.

Aldercar Hall estate was occupied by an old gentleman, a clerk in holy orders, the Rev. John Smith, who used to journey to Nottingham twice a week on horseback and spend the day at his club, and who told my father–with whom he often came and spent an hour–that he once heard John Wesley preach at Nottingham, but it was not so much a sermon, as a recital of the wonderful works of God in different parts of England. In those days my father acted as agent for the Cromford Canal, and lived in the house beside the canal lock, and once, one of my mother's maids was going to take the important journey to Nottingham, and at the station expected to meet an old aunt who acted as housekeeper to an old gentleman named Butler, who lived at Langley. Very soon the girl came back disapointed, her aunt not having turned up. By-and-by the old lady came along in a great fluster, and it appeared she had been to Milnhay crossing to take the train knowing nothing about the station, and thought she could hail the train and get on like passengers did on the coaches. I was present and heard her explanation: 'I seed th' coaches and put my umbrella up, but they wouldna' stop.'

Some people were by no means convinced of the permanency of the railway system. There were three old bachelor brothers who kept a farm at Old Brinsley, and the most enlightened of them once said to me, 'For my part I shall be glad when the trains are done away with and we've got the coaches back again.'

There was another thing which we had not. We had no Post Office.

After I had begun my business life, letters had to be taken to Eastwood to post, and although penny postage was established, we at Langley Mill had to pay One Penny for each letter we received.

At my father's dictation, I wrote a petition and took it round for signature, appealing for a post office. When one was established, the most convenient place which could be found was on the Eastwood side, showing where the business centred. It was kept by an old man named Thomas Grundy.

I have said that the Baptist Chapel was the only place of worship and it remained so until 1870, when the partners of the then firm of Smith & Bowes built a Wesleyan Chapel and presented it to the 'Conference.'

The younger partner, John Gething Bowes, was one of the pioneers of extension in Langley Mill. He died in the prime of life in 1874.

Some years after this, Mr. Beresford Wright, of Aldercar Hall, built the pretty little church at Aldercar.

Note: The above digital transcription from 'Walter Barkers' original Letterpress book is by Harry Riley 2018, and curtesy of John Bayliss B.E.M.

Spectacular charity concert result!

On Friday, 27 October 2017, at the Church of St Michael and All Angels, Underwood, ECMVC were joined by great friends, Sonara Singers in a concert organised in aid of the Progressive Supranuclear Palsy Association. All profits were given to the association.

This spectacular concert of fabulous choral singing raised **over £1,200** for the association – a fantastic result and marvellous reward for organisers, Will and Moira Jones!

Sonara delighted the audience with a fabulous selection of items which included *That's Entertainment, Fly Me To The Moon, And All That Jazz, The Impossible Dream*, a brilliant take on *Sing A Song Of Sixpence* and a gorgeous rendition of George Harrison's *Here Comes The Sun*.

ECMVC sang many favourites including *Stout Hearted Men, Unchained Melody, Anthem from Chess Love Is All Around,* and *Bring Him Home*, from Les Miserables. Their contribution to the concert was rounded off with a new song to their repertoire – the hauntingly beautiful, but very powerful, *If We Only Have Love* by Jaques Brel.

Both choirs were led by the indefatigable Musical Director, Liz Moulder, who was brilliantly supported by Gemma Marshall and Teresa Mills, ECMVC and Sonara respective accompanists.

Richard Moulder was the excellent Master of Ceremonies for the evening.

PSPA Charity Concert—the photographs

On Friday, 27 October 2017, at the Church of St Michael and All Angels, Underwood, ECMVC were joined by great friends, Sonara Singers in a concert organised in aid of the Progressive Supranuclear Palsy Association. All profits were given to the

association. PSP is a progressive neurological condition caused by the premature loss of nerve cells in certain parts of the brain. Over time, this leads to difficulties with balance, movement, vision, speech and swallowing. Symptoms can resemble Parkinson's, Alzheimer's, Stroke or Multiple System Atrophy, with the result that initial misdiagnosis is common. The PSP Association raises funds for much needed research into the condition.

This spectacular concert of fabulous choral singing raised over £1,200 for the association – a fantastic result!

Read more details of this concert.

(All photographs courtesy of Roger Prescote and Paul Atchinson, Eastwood Photographic Society.)

'Just a small selection from the gallery of photos'

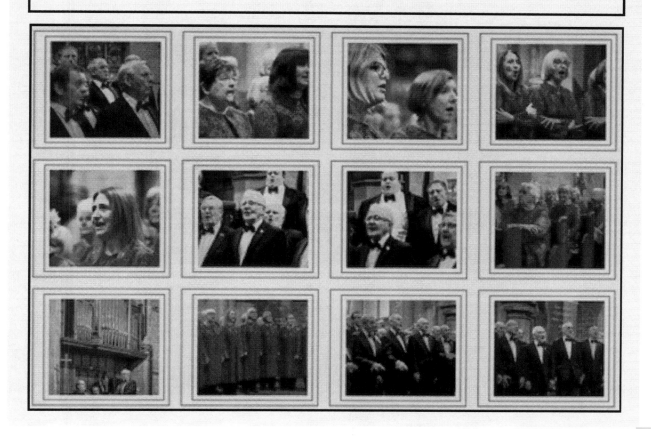

Photo Gallery
Recordings
Listen to our music
Booking the choir

❖ ❖ ❖

//

A tribute to Doreen Lockett
1943– 2017

It was Doreen's funeral: Wednesday 15th Nov. 2017, held at St. Mary's Church Greasley. There are a select few amongst us for whom the description of 'life, death and funeral' is just not enough. Doreen Lockett was surely one of them. Her friendliness, life and passion for people, local history and the church, to name but a few of her many interests, to my mind, far transcended the norm. For those who, like myself, tend to be 'reluctant, believers,' the church's conception and meaning of 'The Holy Spirit' has always seemed no more than a mysterious myth, designed to keep us poor sinners on the straight and narrow.

However, having joined the throng of people who had dropped whatever we were doing, in order to attend this Special Lady's funeral, I followed the crowd into St. Mary's church. And it really was crowded – literally standing room only! The organist later remarked to me that he had never known such a big turnout. There must have been nigh on 300 of us crammed in. There were those present, of course, who'd had the pleasure of knowing her all their lives, as well as people such as I, who had only met her as a 'more than helpful guide' to St. Mary's past church notables, and to local history, particularly those buried in this ancient churchyard.

Yet she always came across like everyone's favourite aunt. 'Doreen's own Spirit of Friendliness' was manifested in this huge congregation; How else can I explain it? She had clearly touched so many lives. With voices raised to the rafters, singing in praise, we could be in no doubt she was still a 'Presence' amongst us. I have been to too many funerals, but never to one quite like this. It was a service and congregation fit for a queen.

Her sudden death and funeral, coming so close to Remembrance Day makes her own poem 'Screen of Remembrance' all the more poignant.

David page: Nov. 2017

The Screen of Remembrance

The chancel screen in loving memory
Tells a story of the true and brave,
Who in the war, to end all wars
For their country – lives they gave.

Never more to walk these fields
Or breathe again the Greasley air,
Instead they died on foreign fields
Where the poppies grow so fair.

From different ranks in regiments
Listed on the screen I see –
A Major, Corporals, Captains, Sergeants
Gunners, Privates and cavalry.

They were fathers, husbands, brothers,
Sons and uncles – neighbours too
Leaving all for King and Country
Achieving peace for me and you.

We all owe a great debt to them,
So read these names as you pass by –
Offer a prayer in grateful thanks
AND MAY THEIR MEMORY NEVER DIE.

Doreen Lockett - May 2014

Donations in lieu of flowers for The Royal British Legion

may be given by retiring collection or sent to:

Gillotts Funeral Directors
154 Nottingham Road, Eastwood, NG16 3GG, Tel: 01773 713484

Interior of Greasley Parish Church of St. Mary.

Service of Thanksgiving
for the life of

Doreen Lockett

1943 – 2017

Tony Harper –

Biography

I have lived in Greasley parish for many years and was born and raised in the adjoining parish of Hucknall. My dad was a coal miner and my brothers and sister worked in the public sector, all of whom live locally. I have a daughter, 29, who is teacher and a son, 28, who is a bank manager. My partner is Dawn, who was raised in Eastwood and Brinsley.

After leaving school I joined the police Service where I rose to the rank of Acting Chief Inspector. I was awarded the Police Good Conduct, Long Service and Queens Jubilee medals. During my 35 years of service I was fortunate to have a varied career including public order, firearms, VIP and royalty protection.

I served for 7 years in the community relations department, where I was involved in community engagement and local council relations and was the force School's and Youth Officer, where I introduced drug education into schools and youth groups, I set up neighbourhood watch schemes. I was trained in public speaking and delivered several Key Note Speeches in London,

My peers elected me as the national chairman of the Police federation Equality Committee, where I frequently met cabinet ministers of all political parties. My priority was for Police Officers to respect the views of all people.

Charity Work

I served for several years on the Princes Trust charity, which was set up to help disadvantaged young people, I set up an after school learning project to redress the imbalance in educational standards, which then became a national project.

I was the national co-ordinator for the 'Crimebeat' charity, which funded young peoples crime prevention projects. I have regularly run quizzes for 'Children In Need' and as a runner I have been sponsored for charities such as local hospitals, dependents trusts and recently Broxtowe Women's charity. I enjoyed being chair of governors at a local village school. I am currently the chair of Eastwood Volunteer Bureau and represent the local council on Eastwood Age Concern.

Interests

I am keen on keeping fit, and am a member of a local gym, I regularly take part in marathons, I am a member of a local running club and represent the police athletics team, I also enjoy long distance walking, cycling and squash. I am a keen F1 fan.

Politics

As a serving police officer I could not be involved in politics even though I had a great interest. Having recently retired I now have the opportunity, time and energy to devote to my passion which is to listen to your views and represent you. I have worked hard to protect our local greenbelt with its rich heritage

I am currently a Parish Councillor on Greasley Parish Council, a Councillor on Broxtowe Borough Council (Eastwood Hall) where I am Chair of Jobs & Economy Committee and a Councillor on Nottinghamshire County Council (Eastwood) where I am Vice Chair of Social Services.

**Councillor
Tony
Harper**

❖❖❖

Part Two

Harry Riley's Review
'The Waterways Festival'
2017 August Bank Holiday

The festival stretched across several fields opposite The Gallows Inn, Nottingham Road Ilkeston, with the added bonus of Free Parking.

Not only that, but this wonderfully well organised open–air event had

A team of car-parking-marshalls equipped with walkie-talkies to guide drivers into clearly defined areas. And to cap it all, we had the most gloriously warm sunshine.

I arrived just before noon, and the festival was already in full swing with live music piped from the large entertainment marquee. There were hundreds of people milling around, soaking up the holiday atmosphere. Dozens of Heritage tents, hot and cold food stalls, vintage cars, motorbikes and caravans, and then as I made my way towards the Erewash Canal, there they all were: gaily decked out narrow boats, moored along the towpath, as far as the eye could see. It made a glorious sight, with the flags and bunting, and all that traditional narrow-boat sign art (in amongst the craft stalls, a signwriter was busy in his tent demonstrating his special skills)

I now made a bee-line for my own particular interest of the day, and soon found the Friends of Bennerley Viaduct. I was informed they are hoping to have a Lottery Grant application ready very shortly. This historic landmark really does need preserving for future generatons to enjoy.

I could have stayed forever on this last day of the festival. Great thanks should go to the organisers, the show participants, the boaters, and especially to the interested public, who made it such a magnificent event.

Early Years

Looking back at my 1950's childhood

Part one. 'Our House'

By Trevor Belshaw

I was born in Ilkeston, Derbyshire, on a cold, wet December night in 1953. My father was an ex RAF man who was too young for the war, but had to join to do his national service. My mother was a former machinist in the rag trade. We lived in a house owned by the Iron Works company, where my father, grandfather and most of the town were employed.

The old house was Victorian, set in the centre of a terraced block. It was built from red brick and had a dirty slate roof which leaked when it rained. Two up-two down in style, it got to be a little bit crowded with four kids in one bedroom and mum and dad in the other. At the top of the stairs sat a metal bucket to catch any water that seeped through the roof. If the rain was heavy, we used to place bowls and saucepans strategically around the upstairs rooms to catch the dripping water. We had an enamel chamber pot in each bedroom called 'the po' which would be deposited into the bucket after use to keep the already damp air in the bedroom a little fresher. My father (thankfully) emptied the thing every morning before we were up

Downstairs we had the 'back room' with the big black range for cooking. The floor was red tile, set on earth with a square mat in the centre. On the rug sat a solid oak table with six chairs tucked neatly underneath, it's worn, well-scrubbed surface covered with a clean white cloth. On either side of the range was a pair of moth eaten armchairs, the backs of the chairs were covered with embroidered cloth. In front of the range was a peg rug which held a dog and two kids comfortably. As there were four of us, two always had to sit at the table to listen to an ancient radio set that would decide which channel we listened to no matter where we set it on the dial.

There was a large built-in cupboard next to the range which held an extra tablecloth, spare plates, mum's sewing box and a host of other important, but little used possessions.

On the back wall, opposite the range, was a huge dresser with plates on the shelves and cutlery in the drawers. The bottom cupboards were filled with our meagre book collection and the family games compendium. We got a TV set when I was about five, a huge old mahogany box with a tiny screen in the front. I hate to think how much it cost my parents to rent, but it was the thing to have. The neighbours had one, so we needed one too.

I remember singing along to 'Watch With Mother'. 'Bill and Ben' were great, as were 'The Woodentops'. I never did get on with 'Andy Pandy' though; there was something strange about him.

The front room was the 'best room' and held a polished table with four soft seated chairs. Either side of the open fire place sat two wing backed armchairs with delicate lace head covers. The room had a good carpet with only two-feet of floor showing around its edges. On the back wall was a china cabinet which showed off the best teacups, plates and one or two small ornaments. The mantelpiece held the clock and for some reason, a letter rack. At either end were tall brass candlesticks, unencumbered by candles.

On a small table under the window sat a bible. Every house had one. I had one of my own, won like Tom Sawyer's at a Sunday school prize giving. I didn't have to collect tickets for mine; I just answered a few questions about Jesus.

We weren't allowed in the front room, not even on a Sunday. It was reserved for Christmas day or whenever my mother's parents visited. They owned their own house up in town, had a car and only came to visit a few times a year.

The front door opened onto the front door step; a wide red block that was polished heartily and religiously every week. Great pride was taken over how good that step looked. You could see your face on ours. Every step was inspected by other residents of the street as they passed; I think the saying went something like, 'dirty step, dirty house'. I suspect that even people who did own a dirty house kept their front step clean; it was a badge of honour.

Strangely, the front door was never used. Even officials and royalty like my grandparents came in through the back door. The rent man came around the back, as did every other visitor we had, including the 'nit nurse' and the midwife.

At the back of the house was the outhouse/washroom and pantry. The room was long and narrow with the customary leaky roof. The wind used to whistle through the gap under the door. We used to place an old coat on the floor to plug the gap when it got particularly bad. At one end was a huge white sink that would hold a child quite easily. I know because I was bathed in it until I was four.

Along one wall was a cupboard containing washing powder, soap, carbolic and some other evil smelling stuff. The floor tile and front step polish, was kept in there along with a variety of cockroach, silverfish, ant, and insect killing powders. I can remember a can of DDT too. I think we used to de-flea the dog with it.

We had fly paper hanging in most rooms through the summer months. I remember quite vividly, the night a dead fly fell from its sticky trap onto my portion of once a month, homemade fruit cake. I struggled to find it among the raisins, but I wasn't going to let it put me off my pudding. I was sick that night but I think it was more the thought of eating the thing than any actual ailment. Mouse traps were hidden under the dresser, china cabinet and radio and were emptied of their contents almost daily.

The pantry had a stone, cold shelf for meat and a row of shelves for tinned and boxed food. On rare occasions there might be a couple of rashers of bacon sat alongside a kipper or a skinned, boned rabbit waiting to be shown the pot. Mostly though, there was a lump of something that my dad used to call 'scrag end.' I hated that pantry. There was nothing much in the way of exciting food in there anyway, but the sight of the rabbit or scrag-end horrified me. I used to have nightmares if I was sent in there to get the uncut loaf and pat of margarine. I didn't eat meat, even in my early years. As soon as I realised that a portion of rabbit or lamb was previously a real living, breathing animal, I flatly refused to have anything to do with it. At the butcher's shop at the top of the road they used to have rabbits hanging on a rail outside. I remember embarrassing my mother by yelling at the butcher, demanding he let them go; I had no idea they were already dead. As I've grown older I have learned to understand why people eat meat, I don't get angry about it but it still isn't for me.

On the back of the solid-outhouse door hung a tin bath. It was toss up on bath night as to who got in first. The water had to be heated in a copper boiler, (a large metal tank that would be filled using saucepans.) Bath night was normally a Saturday, as it meant we were clean for Sunday school the next morning. None of us were really that keen, there was always a draught, but the first in got the hottest and cleanest water. No one wanted to go in after my youngest brother, because he always peed in it.

The back door was never locked to my knowledge. I can't remember a key ever being in the lock and there were certainly no bolts. I doubt it was left open because there was no fear of burglary in those days, I think it was simply that we had nothing worth stealing. Every other day our neighbour would walk in as though it were her house and ask to borrow a cup of sugar for her husband's tea. Sometimes a chunk of bread or a little pat of margarine went with her too. I honestly can't remember anything ever being returned, but it didn't seem to matter and the subject was never brought up, at least not when we kids were about.

After the Flood
(part two of looking back at my 1095's childhood by Trevor Belshaw)

In the early 1960's we moved from our old Victorian slum to a brand new house on a brand new estate in Kirk Hallam. Ilkeston. I was about seven at the time The old house, which was tied to my father's job at the iron works had been flooded. We lost just about everything; the waters had come half way up the stairs.

The flood struck on Sunday 4th December 1960. The normally placid Nutbrook stream, swollen by heavy rain, burst its banks and flooded the Ironworks and the bottom half of Crompton Street. The water carried a hidden danger in the form of highly flammable, Benzoline oil that sat on the surface of the water. I didn't know until years later that the oil had been a problem. I remember my father sitting on the sill of the upstairs window of our house as he smoked and chatted to the people next door while we waited for help. Cigarette stubs were flicked into the water at regular intervals.

We were rescued by the fire brigade who took us all to a community centre where we slept in sleeping bags on the floor for a few nights.

It was a major adventure for us kids but not so much fun for the parents or the older members of the community. I could have slept on a clothes line in those days but I doubt some people there got a wink of sleep.

We were fed soup and sandwiches by the Salvation Army. Before the evening meal we all had to stand and sing 'I'll be a sunbeam.' My father, a reluctant Christian at best, would move his lips like a poor ventriloquist then burst into song on the final line of the chorus.

A sunbeam, a sunbeam,

Jesus wants me for a sunbeam;

A sunbeam, a sunbeam,

A bloody fine sunbeam am I.

During the day we played Beetle, Draughts, Snakes and Ladders and Monopoly. The adult members of our little community must have been sick to death of Ludo, but they gritted their teeth and played on. The situation reminded many of them about the nights they spent, huddled together, sheltering from the German bombs some twenty years before. Hours spent hunched over a Ludo board must have been a chore, but I think they'd have done anything to keep the more energetic kids on their backsides, sat on chairs at tables instead of hurtling around on the parquet floor.

In the evenings we stayed up well beyond our usual bedtime and played 'Beggar my Neighbour', 'Snap' and 'Happy Families'. At nine thirty we were strip-washed in the totally inadequate toilet block before joining a queue to be given a mug of Ovaltine. After that, three quarters of the lights were turned out and we would go to sleep while our parents sat at the top end of the hall, discussing the future with their peers.

After a few days we were split up. Some of us went to stay with Aunty Kath and Uncle John in their new house. They used to live on the same street as us but had managed to get a move to a new council house a few months before. They weren't real relatives; we used to call every woman on the street 'Aunty,' back then. The youngest two went with Mum and Dad to stay at Grandad's. He was a very strict old man and I never really did hit it off with him. He couldn't understand my reluctance to eat meat. In his day you ate what you were given or you starved. We weren't disciplined enough for him either. Anyway, I was glad I got to go to Aunty Kath's, they had no children of their own and we were spoilt rotten while we were there.

Our family was reunited when we moved to Abbot Road in Kirk Hallam. The new house had everything the old one didn't have, including a gas fire, a gas cooker, an electric immersion heater for hot water, a garden with real soil instead of old soot, and a roof that didn't leak. We felt we had made a step up.

The school was about the same distance away but now we could get a bus instead of having to walk. There were new shops that sold a wide variety of goods, instead of the one, damp, smelly old shop that only sold a limited number of items. We had a newsagent, a hardware store and a CO-OP supermarket. The estate was only part built; we were one of the first families to move in. We were surrounded by green fields, trees and hedgerows. A crystal clear brook meandered across the field at the back of us. We could catch frogs, newts and sticklebacks, creatures we had only ever seen in books before.

To top it all, we had three bedrooms, which meant two if us shared a room instead of all four being crammed into one. (When we were very young, three of us used to share one ancient double bed.) The mood in the house was completely different; we had more space and although it was still very difficult to find a place to be alone, it was so much better than before. There was no damp, no silverfish, no mousetraps and no chance of meeting a large, brown rat when you ventured out onto the back yard. There were no more Saturday nights sat in an old tin bath while a howling wind whistled under the gap in the back door; now we had a real bathroom with a real bath and best of all, an inside toilet.

All the lights worked, we had power sockets to spare. Mum and Dad got lots of new appliances, I assume they rented some and bought others on the never-never. Just about everyone rented TVs from Curry's or Rediffusion; the latter also wired radio into houses. You could rent a washing machine too; we had a twin tub, (a washing machine and a spin drier in one unit,) at the old house everything was done by hand in the big sink in the scullery.

Amazingly the big old radio set still worked. We had found it floating around the stairwell with the dog sat on top the morning of the flood. Dad took it upstairs and dried it out. When we plugged it in at the new house it fired up first time. Reassuringly, it still decided what random station it would play, it always had, no matter what we set it to on the dial.

The big old wooden cabinet TV hadn't fared so well and never worked again after its watery experience. My dad said he was sad to see it go as it had the ghost of Logie Baird inside the cabinet. We all thought he meant Yogi Bear so we were very sorry to see it go too. The new set made up for it though. It had a screen four times the size of the old one and we could sit at the back of the room and still see the Woodentops or Huckleberry Hound.

The houses around us were still being built. Wimpey, the company building them, used to boast, that they completed a house in a day. I can believe it too. On the way to school in the morning there would be a set of brick footings on the opposite side of the street and when we got back in the afternoon there would be virtually a whole house standing there. I discovered how the miracle worked during our school holidays, the workmen would bolt pre-cast concrete panels together, and in a matter of hours the bare brick footings had become the shell of a house. I'm still impressed when I think of how quickly those places were put together. They are all still inhabited now, fifty years on.

The bottom of the street was turned over to private houses. They were made of mostly brick and each had a small wall at the front. Every house had a garage for parking cars that the vast majority of them didn't own. When we lived in the old house on Crompton Street there were only two car owners, and as one of those was a sales rep it was only really there at the weekend. The other was a 1930s Ford which was parked at the back of a property and hadn't been started in all the time I lived there. We kids used to play at gangsters or cops and robbers in it. Our street on the new estate boasted at least half a dozen cars and it was no longer an event to see one drive off, although any child fortunate enough to belong to a car owning family was classed as being posh.

I will never forget my time in the old slum house by the ironworks. Life was hard, very hard at times and we had so little. What we did have though, was imagination, a steely determination and a comradery that would see us through most of what life could throw at us. In the new house we breathed clean air and we were ill a lot less. The kids with chest complaints who used to struggle to join in many of our games, could suddenly run all day long. We did get sick but were well again in days, not weeks.

Instead of playing on the filthy coal dust and chemical-covered land between the iron works and the coke ovens, we now had an expanse of hills and fields to explore. We learned to climb trees, we discovered, (to my eternal shame,) bird nesting, we built dens in the copses and woods, we played football on grass. In the holidays we went out in a morning and weren't seen again until early evening. We walked miles; we were explorers, searching out territories for future generations of children. I went back recently; most of it is built on now, though there are still some pockets of grassland and the odd cluster of trees to be found.

It's a shame. Kids deserve the freedom to wander and explore. My own children never had to walk five miles to see a working windmill, we used to take them in the car. They did get to see the countryside, but we had to take them further afield to find it.

D. H. Lawrence, Eastwood and District in the Last Century

Emerging from the grimy, coal-dusted streets of Eastwood, into the fresh, clean air and golden tranquillity of the hills and valleys of Amber, Erewash and Beauvale, it is easy to see, even today, well over a century later, why the young David Herbert Lawrence was so enraptured by this rural idyll, literally on his doorstep, and why he so willingly embraced all that meant life and living.

For he knew first hand just what his own father, and fellow mine-workers had to go through each day as they toiled for 10 and 12 hours or more, crouched deep underground, ripping out the black underbelly of the earth, and what it did to them and their women folk, making them old before their time.

With his friends at Haggs farm here was what he craved for: the flora and forna, and constancy of farming, where life was regularly reproducing itself.

Lawrence, with his sharpened senses, poet's-eyes and ears, keenly attuned to his surroundings, would have surely felt in the noisy silence, the ghostly echos of the Carthusian monks of Beauvale Priory, still toiling in the fields, and he would have also taken in the contrasting, fine living that went on in the big houses of wealthy land owners up and down the country, with their lavish decadent, parties that went on for days and days, with no expense spared, and all paid for on the backs of the workers, such as his own kith and kin. This is what must surely have shaped his writings and unfettered his imagination, giving him the creativity and freedom to abandon the prudish and puritanical rules laid down by established society and to give vent to that unbridled passion we see in 'Lady Chatterley's Lover,' that so shocked, disgusted, appalled, infuriated, intrigued, excited, and fascinated those staid Victorian Ladies in their genteel drawing rooms, perhaps in equal measure.

'Oh, how could anyone write such sensuous filth, and blasthemy, reducing human behaviour to that of the beasts in the fields; do we know of anyone who has a copy?'

Such was the outcry, that Lawrence was shunned by polite society and the brilliance of his work went unrecognised and was even banned for decades. He knew, he must have known

The startling effect his extraordinary, sexually explicit novels would have had on female readers, and their male partners, and yet he clearly did not care if he was to be banished–ostracized; he'd suffered that already, for political reasons, and now, from across the world he would lay bare the hypocrisy of Victorian England, which dictated that anything, with the slightest hint of a sexual nature should be covered up and hidden from view, even to the extent of draping lace covers over curvacious wooden table, or piano legs.

Impressionable minds of either sex should not be exposed to naked flesh, beyond that of the female ankle; never mind what their elders and betters were getting up to behind closed doors in those affluent mansions on grand estates. Too much intimate knowledge of the body was not to be tolerated, especially amongst the lower classes, for who knows what it might lead to; no, we couldn't have that, it would have been too distressing for the established order.

Harry Riley.

Following the very sad and sudden death of Ms. Doreen Lockett, (this publication's guide to St. Mary's Church Greasley, to the noteble people buried there, and to Greasley's past history) it was beholden upon yours truly (Harry Riley) to try and locate another reliable source of historical fact about that particular district. Then, quite by chance, a superb website fulfilled all we could wish for in our brief digest. It was Andy Nicholson's: 'Nottinghamshire History.

'Website: www.nottshistory.org.uk

Andy, who now lives in North Wales, was until two years ago a resident of Newthorpe and he has willingly made his research into North Notts., freely available to local history buffs such as ourselves. This is wonderful information, especially as much of this 'older history is not yet so readily available on the Internet in digital format.

I refer particularly to a book published by Rodolph Baron Von Huber, Vicar of Greasley, in 1901 and entitled: GRISELIA in SNOTINGHSCIRE. Dipping into the section of this venerable fount of ancient knowledge we learn that Moorgreen was once part of Greasley Castle Estate with thatched cottages. However, owing to Earl Cowper's beneficience, later-day architecture has provided new dwellings of very pleasing and picturesque architecture.

For several generations The Barber family (local colliery owners) built up and extended Lambclose House, stables, grounds and shruberies, Mr. Thomas Barber turning the premises into a fine country house, surounded by woodland and now containing a lake known as Moorgreen Reservoir. It was built by the Great Northern Railway and Mr. Thomas Barber once had a steam-houseboat on the water for the benefit of his family and guests. These days it is stocked with fish for a private angling association.

Mr. Thomas Barber's eldest son: Mr. Thomas Philip Barber had been a County Councillor who fought in the Boer War as an officer with the South Notts Hussars Yeomanry. Another interesting fact about the Barber family is that the widow of the late Mr. Thomas Barber was a descendent of Admiral Sir Edward Spragge, mentioned in Samual Pepys Diaries as a distinguished naval commander who perished in a boat which was sunk in action with Van Tromp in 1673.

Beauvale Priory ruins are now in the care of English Heritage and within the grounds of a private farm, currently owned by Mr. and Mrs Whyte. They have restored the gatehouse, making it open to the public as a busy, high quality Tea Rooms. They also hold fairs and festivals in the grounds.

Andy Nicholson covers the fascinating history of those silent Carthusian Monks of Beauvale Priory and their Priors, martered to King Henry the eighth, during the reformation.

Beauvale Priory Ruins now in the care of English Heritage and situated on private farmland.

The Barber's Home: Lambclose House: all 3 photo's from Andy Nicholson's nottshistory.org.uk

Mr. Thomas Barber

Mr. Philip Barber

The Oak Leaf military motif of the South Notts Hussar's Cap Badge

[This item belonging to Gunner Page]

Beauvale Priory Ruins now in the care of English Heritage and situated on private farmland.

'Moor Green Reservoir' owned by Great Northern Railway. Mr. T. Barber once had a steam boat on this water. Photo from Andy Nicholson's nottshistory.org.uk

◄ Left: Beauvale House, Moorgreen: built 1873 for Earl Cowper and thought to be the setting for D.H. lawrence's Lady Chatterley's Lover

Horse & Groom Pub Moorgreen

Bottom two photo's also from Andy Nicholson's nottshistory.org.uk

The Barber's Home: Lambclose House: all 3 photo's from Andy Nicholson's nottshistory.org.uk

Mr. Thomas Barber

Mr. Philip Barber

The Oak Leaf military motif of the South Notts Hussar's Cap Badge

[This item belonging to Gunner Page]

'PARTY PIECES'
By Helen Sharp

Can you remember the wonderful parties we used to have at school in the late '40's and early '50's, especially at Christmas, and even at the end of July when the school year finished.

Many things were still on ration, so we all took different items of food that could be spared from the Co-op weekly order.

Even items that had been squirrelled away to the back of the cupboard, say a jelly; if possible a small tin of fruit, or maybe some spam. A lovely home-made loaf or a sponge cake was very welcome, and perhaps even a tin of evaporated milk. Sometimes a tasty dish of cream cheese, made from sour milk, which had hung over the sink on a hook from the ceiling in a muslin bag. It had been mixed together with a good pinch of salt and left to drip away until only the curds were left. What remained made delicious sandwiches, on its own or together with water-cress, picked fresh from the streams and brooks, which in those days ran crystal-clear. Occasionally there might be lettuce fresh from the garden, or home-grown beetroot straight from the ground. Potted meat or 'potted dog' as I knew it, was gorgeous on crusty bread, with a little butter mixed together with margarine, or as we called it 'maggy-ann.

Polonni or black pudding; I'd better not tell you the names we gave them, (but here's a clue: 'Red D***' and 'Donkey's Pl******'). You know; looking back, there were quite a few families who brought food that I wished I hadn't eaten. Many 'Dripping' or 'Lard' sandwiches were consumed from people, well, let's just say now, I wished they hadn't bothered. Never mind, I'm still here, so they can't have been that bad. But, Yuk! Let's change the subject.

All those home-made jam and lemon curd tarts with lovely crumbly pastry, if your mum was a good pastry cook, or if she wasn't, maybe you would take home some of those horrible, greasy, variable coloured and textured, soggy or hard cheese straws in the most peculiar shapes imaginable.

All those delicacies were sorted out before the day, so that we never had too much of one thing when the time came. All the sandwiches were made at home. Assorted, pre-made puddings, were lovingly carried, as though they were priceless works of art, to school for the feast. If we were lucky, lovely coloured trifles covered in hundreds and thousands, together with little silver balls, that just about smashed your teeth to bits when you tried to eat them, also appeared on the day, in different shapes, along with the red, yellow and green jellies. Strawberry and chocolate blancmanges; a few biscuits might arrive too: normally, Arrowroot, Rich Tea, or Morning Coffee; by that I mean they were usually plain but, we didn't care, they were sweet, what more could you ask for. Very often, after all the 'goodies' were laid out in a cool class room, some kind soul would go along the line and try most of the puddings, just with one finger's worth; but did we care? 'Course not!

On the actual day, or maybe on the night before, cupboards and drawers were raided. Utensils were needed, dishes, together with plates, and each item had to be marked with it's own secret mark, that only you would recognise–you hoped! Woe betide you if you didn't know your own stuff. It was just after the war you know, so you were taught to respect anything that belonged to the household. The family had to work hard to get the money to pay for anything, and the phrase we always heard was: 'They don't grow on trees you know.' And it is still used today!

So with that in mind, a spot of paint, usually a horrible dark green gloss (I think it must have been cheap) was dabbed on the bottom of your plate (chipped of course) dish (likewise) and the same with the cup. Now here was a problem, most folk in those days had the same colour paint. I suppose it was used in the 'Blackout'. So the paint had to be put on the pots somehow different to anyone else's. Maybe a picture, or a flower; a house, but mainly an initial.

I remember I mostly took an enamel mug, plate and dish, by kind permission of my Uncle George and the 'Grenadier Guards'. So much more practical and a lot easier to transport and bash about. This was after all, our infant and junior school, not that much care was taken, I can assure you.

Hopefully the paint had been applied at least the night before, otherwise you could find your pots, enamel or not, sticking to the coloured crepe paper, laid out on the tables as tablecloths.

Then we come to the cutlery, these were not painted, oh no. The sewing box or work basket came into being. Different coloured wools of different thicknesses were used. All socks were wool then and usually home-knitted, so plenty of wool left over for darning the socks, whether for work or best. If the wool was for work socks to be worn down the pits, the colours didn't always match the sock.

Lengths of one colour were cut from the main ball and wrapped around the stem of the spoon and fork, 'can't ever remember taking a knife. If an unusual colour was not forthcoming, then out would come my paint-box and paint would be smeared over the wool. Not only to colour it but also to seal it, so as not to fray.

Games would be played after the tea. Nothing boisterous. We didn't get much rich food at this point in history so stomachs were rather sensitive, but there was always someone who would part with their tea all over the rest of us.

It was always a very exciting day as I remember and was thoroughly enjoyed by the kids, if not by the teachers. We would all go home worn out, still arguing about whose mother had made the best food. Looking forward to next year, and to do it all over again.

Do you know, I've forgotten something very important: 'Party-hats,' and at Christmas, coloured decorations, which we thought were very pretty. We made these in class weeks before in readyness for the celebrations. All made of paper of course. The hat was like an upside down boat that sat on your head, or maybe a crown with bright jewels painted around the rim.

Again all made of old newspaper, painted with thick water paint, so wet it took them ages to dry out. There were paper Chinese Lanterns too, very pretty and effective. Last but not least your place name, written in your very best handwriting

All these things were held together with a folur and water paste that got everywhere. This was your Bostick of the '40's, but by gum, it was messy. None the less it did it's job and did it well.

So at the end of a very long week and a very exciting day we would all trundle home. Not without our hats and lanterns clutched in our sticky hands. They might come in useful for Christmas at home. You never know.

'Brown Never Black'

the year.

Meetings are held on the 2nd Wednesday of the month 1pm – 3.30pm at the Catholic Church hall, Hill Top, 280, Nottingham Road, Eastwood,

By Helen Sharp

I want you to cast your mind back for a few minutes…to a time when your parents chose your shoes. A time when you had no say in the matter. A time when it was what they could afford as well as what was in the shops. Let me tell you how it was for me and my friends.

A few years ago, AHEM, when I was a little girl, I always seemed to have brown shoes. Heavy brown leather ones with a thick sole and very solid heel. The tops were also very sturdy, with brown laces that were always coming undone. "Fasten your shoes up , you'll fall over them" or "Tie your laces properly." Doing up these laces of course was no easy task, not to a young child. When I started school if you couldn't do up your own laces you had to wear some other form of shoe.'Can't remember 'slip-ons' so it must have been sandals. These were also usually brown in colour, that fastened with a buckle on the side of the instep. No troublesome laces, but these buckles were sewn on, and of course the stitching would come undone just at the wrong moment and off the damn buckle would come, lost forever on the school field or in the corridor when changing classrooms, never to be seen again.

These sandlas were all very well, but they lacked an attachment, you either loved or hated −'**Segs'** What joy they brought to some! Who could make their heels give off the most sparks in the playground or on the pavement?

These segs were put onto our heels to supposedly make the shoes last longer. 'Not sure whether they worked or not. I think it was a ruse by the makers to sell more of them , because the segs themselves didn't seem to make the she last any longer. It was also a weekly chore for the dads to knock a few more segs in. My, what a noise they made too: Clunk, Scrape, Clunk, every time your foot was lowered to the floor, or should I say dragged across the surface. On Sunday nights out would come the old hobbling iron and dad on his hands and knees with the packet of segs in one hand and a hammer in the other and then the banging would start. First a couple of little taps then two or three bangs, segs in the right place around the heel. Job done for another week!

Sometimes these shoes or sandals were not brown at all but 'Ox Blood,' what a name for a colour. I've not heard of it for years thank goodness. It was a nice shade of red though. It depended on what colour Cherry Blossom or Kiwi Boot Polish was in use at your house at the time, that determined the outcome. Nothing must be wasted, so no good moaning about it. Maybe Monday, brown, and by Friday, Ox Blood. 'Bit like having a new pair really.

Parents always cleaned their children's shoes, until they were old enough to do them themselves, that is. They had to be taken off as soon as you reached home and neatly placed at the side of the door to be picked up next morning, clean and shiny. No child in my village would ever be seen with dirty, scuffed shoes. No, I exaggerate. There were families that only had a bath or a wash and that included their hair, when the *Nit-Nurse* came round or it was time for our medical examinations. Mind you these were few and far between but they did exist. But back to the shoes. The soles of their shoes were often made of cardboard. Put inside to try and fool people. Of course the packing would be worn out on the walk to school but, the worst thing was when it rained, it just fell to pieces as soon as their feet touched the floor. We all knew about it but no one would comment in case our own shoes wore out before the **Provident Cheque man** brought a new voucher so new ones could be bought. Then all was well with the world as well as your feet.

When the time drew near for this event, many kids and I include myself in this, would hope and pray for a pair of wonderful, posh 'Black 'shoes. I can't remember any coming my way. Never mind, at least I had shoes.

Winter brought in an entirely new set of rules. Wellingtons or wellies as we knew them. These were always worn when it rained or snowed. I hated the damn things. Always having had very thin legs there was more than enough room at the top of the legs-you know what i'm going to say don't you. The top of the said wellie always flapped around my calf and of course, by the time school was reached that tide mark band was a bright red-raw ring right round my leg. We girls didn't wear long socks, so it was worse for us. Having reached school these were changed for the smelliest, dirtiest, ill- fitting footwear imaginable. What do I mean? Why, pumps, slippers, plimsolls, whatever you want to call them. These were kept in cages in the school corridor (best place for them). A pair was given to you when you first started in the infants, and given back when you left, they fitted you, in a fashion then, but oh, the smell. Sometimes the poorer children of the village borrowed them and wore them for home. Again not many, but there were always the few that did. Being passed on from pupil to pupil, goodness knows how many feet had been in them before yours, Verruca's? never heard of 'em, and did we bother? No, we weren't fussy, couldn't afford to be, could we.

Helen Sharp.

The Nottingham West Breathe Easy group is just one of more than 230 across the country which are all part of the British Lung Foundation's support network. The BLF is the only UK charity working on behalf of all those with lung disease. We have been running for over 8 years now in Eastwood.
We offer support, advice, information on living with and self managing a lung condition. It is also a chance to meet and socialise with people in a similar situation. The group is open to all those who fight for breath, their

families and carers as a result of a lung condition Just come along and join a really friendly fun group. We have a lunch club to start the monthly meeting, and a variety of medical, social and local interest talks. We also hold local fund raising events and raise awareness throughout NG16 2AQ

Car parking in the church

Breathe Easy Nottingham West's also hold a twice weekly specially adapted **Respiratory exercise classes** to help control breathlessness, boost confidence levels and well-being. Classes are seated or standing held at different levels depending on ability at Plumptre Hall, Church Street, Eastwood on Tuesday and Thursday's 11-12 All Welcome £3.50

Singing Group Meet every wednesday 2.30-3.30 (Every 2nd wednesday 3pm-3.45 because of support group joining in)

There's increasing evidence that singing regularly, and as part of a group, can help physically, psychologically and socially. Singing exercises the heart and lungs and provides excellent health benefits to everyone especially if you have a lung conditions. People say singing is uplifting and joyful. They feel positive during the singing session – and the positive mood continues afterwards. Singing can help if you feel depressed, stressed or anxious. It is not a choir , you don't have to be able to sing

How much does it cost? Answer a £3 or donation Includes a cuppa

OPEN TO ALL JUST COME ALONG

JUST COME AND ENJOY A GOOD OLD SINGALONG

Speakers list for Breathe Easy 2018

JANUARY 10th Living with oxygen Julie Owens & Loise Bolton

FEBURARY 14thNational energy action. Adam Lever Everyone Health

MARCH 14th Ann Featherstone From the music Hall to dog dramas; Entertaining the Victorians.

APRIL 11th Exercise and why it's a life saver Lynn Davey

MAY 9th Wiltshire foods demo and tasting

JUNE 13th David Coleman 'The famous Pitman'

JULY 11th Cream Tea and social

AUGUST 8th Dr Lim our local GP

SEPTEMBER 12th Tax care and Toyboys

OCTOBER 10th Nurses question and answer session
NOVEMBER 14th TBC
DECEMBER 12th FUDDLE and Singalong

If you wish to know more about Breathe Easy Nottingham West please contact
Jane Reeve 07516 493459 or Teresa Burgoyne 07809 430616 If you wish to know more about the British Lung Foundation, Website : http://www.lunguk.org or phone the BLF Helpline: 03000 030 555

**Easy Breathe Nottingham West
Christmas 2017 Dinner preparations
at the Hilltop Priory Church Hall**

the age of 22, he was a third mate on a Liverpool tea clipper involved in trade with China.

In 1862, Pickering became disenchanted with the sea and, imbued with a

❖ ❖ ❖

A Man for all Seasons

William Alexander Pickering (born 9 June 1840, Eastwood, Nottinghamshire, England–died January 1907, San Remo, Italy) was the first Protector of Chinese in Singapore. He joined the British colonial administration in 1877 and was the first British officer who could speak and write Chinese. He was also fluent in the Mandarin dialects, having worked for over two decades in China. As the first Protector of Chinese, he worked to eradicate the abuses of the <u>coolie</u> (unskilled labourer) trade, regulate secret society activities and arbitrate their conflicts, as well as establish an Office of Virtue (called *Poh Leung Kuk* in Cantonese) for the prevention of child prostitution.

<u>Fascination with all things Chinese</u>

The sixth child and only son in a family of eight, Pickering was born in Eastwood, Nottinghamshire. He received his education at a private school in Nottingham and at 16 years old, embarked on a career at sea. He became an apprentice on board an East Indiaman vessel that sailed the ports of China, Burma (Myanmar), Siam (Thailand) and the Malay archipelago.1 By strong curiosity about the Chinese, became a tide-waiter (an officer who boards anchored vessels to take stock of imports and exports) with the Chinese imperial maritime custom service on Pagoda island. The island was located on the River Min, near Foochow in Fujian Province, China. He took the opportunity to learn the Foochow dialect and spent a quarter of his salary to hire a native speaker to teach him Mandarin.

Given his knowledge of Chinese and Mandarin dialects, Pickering was asked to accompany Mr Maxwell, the newly appointed commissioner of customs for Formosa, to the southern Chinese ports to establish custom houses in 1863. There, Pickering went on expeditions up the coast to arrest vessels that were conducting illicit trade at forbidden ports. In order to identify these illegal vessels, he communicated with local fishermen in their native languages or dialects. In 1865, Pickering was given charge of the customs at Anping, the port of Taiwanfoo, Formosa. In 1867, he moved on to take charge of the Taiwanfoo branch of an English firm, Messrs McPhail & Co. Plagued by fever and chronic dysentery, Pickering returned to England for a year's leave at the end of 1870.

Making his mark: ending the dispute in Larut

Pickering met Sir Harry St George Ord (Governor of the Straits Settlements from 1867–1873) during his leave in London. Finding Pickering fluent in the Chinese language, St George offered him the position of Chinese Interpreter to the Straits Settlements Government. When Pickering arrived iSingapore in March 1872 to assume the post, he was the only European officer in the service of the Settlements who could speak Chinese. He set about to ensure that official interpretations and translations were performed correctly, and removed many corrupt court interpreters who had connections with secret societies.

Pickering rose to prominence after successfully settling long-standing disputes between two secret societies, the Ghee Hin and Hai San, over tin mines in Perak, Malaysia during the Larut Wars (1861 to 1873). Pickering was sent to Penang to meet with the relevant Chinese leaders, persuading them individually to a peaceful co-existence in the tin mines in Larut. He persuaded them to resolve their disputes under British arbitration, which led to the signing of the Pangkor Treaty in January 1874. Pickering was also involved in the Pacification Commission that followed in 1875, which accorded different tin mine territories to the two secret societies.

Singapore's first Protector of Chinese The 1870s was a decade of riots and unrest in Singapore, caused largely by the Chinese secret societies. Faced with the need to police the growing Chinese population, Pickering was appointed the first Protector of Chinese on 3rd May 1877, and was given a Chinese shophouse on North Canal Road for the office of the Protectorate of Chinese. One of his immediate tasks was to keep in check the large number of Chinese immigrants arriving in Singapore and to eradicate the abuses of the coolie trade. One measure was to inform the *sinkhehs* (newly arrived coolies) of the presence of the protectorate, encouraging them to approach it when they required help. Pickering did this through interviewing all arriving Chinese immigrants about their circumstances when they disembarked. He stipulated that coolie brokers and coolie depots (where coolies were held while awaiting transport to their assigned work sites) had to be licensed. He also supervised the re-distribution of some of these immigrants to neighbouring regions in Southeast Asia.

Pickering was concurrently made a Registrar of Societies in 1877. He believed that governing the Chinese was the most pressing problem confronting the government, and recognised that control of the Chinese population would require control of the Chinese secret societies. Working through the societies, he made their headmen the channels through which government regulations were passed down, and had them punish law offenders who were their members themselves. Pickering also acted as the mediator for disputes between societies. Any headman who refused to cooperate with the protectorate was banished from Singapore. Gradually, the protectorate supplanted the societies in settling financial and domestic disputes for the Chinese population.

In 1878, with the help of prominent Chinese and European missionary agencies, Pickering established the Office for the Preservation of Virtue, which operated a refuge for women who had fallen victim to prostitution. Women who took shelter there were taught domestic chores, and learned to read and write Chinese in preparation for marriage. Those who married were ensured a recourse should they be ill-treated by their husbands.

The final assault The secret societies perceived Pickering's regulatory measures as an interference in their affairs. On 18 July 1887, a Teochew carpenter, Chua Ah Siok (also spelt as Chua Ah Sioh or Choa Ah Siok), approached Pickering at his office under the guise of presenting a petition, and suddenly hurled an axe at his forehead.15 Pickering did not recover fully from the attack despite repeated extensions of leave, and permanently retired in 1890. He died in San Remo, Italy, in January 1907.

Author
Irene Lim
Credits: Singapore Infopedia

**William Alexander Pickering of Eastwood Notts:
Born June 1840 : Died: San Remo (Italy) Jan: 1907**

William A. PICKERING

PIONEERING IN FORMOSA

Elibron Classics

❖❖❖

Bill Gregory
Born 1922- Died 2017
(My Sporting Memories)

Over the years I have contributed an enjoyable part of my life to the sporting scene in Eastwood, in the shape of Football and cricket.

With football it has been due to my lifelong support of **Nottingham Forest F.C.** And with cricket, my 70 year association with **Eastwood Town Cricket Club,** however, more of cricket later.

My father took me to my first Forest match when I was eight years old in 1930 and I still remember the names of the Forest team that played. fast forward to the post-second-world-war-period and we had formed the Forest Sportsmens Club in Eastwood and I became the secretary for forty glorious years: 1950-1990. We had more than 200 members in the club and Forest had two great managers in those forty years: Billy Walker during the first ten years and Brian Clough in the final twenty years. That first decade saw Forest go from third division to first division and in 1959 we took over 200 supporters by train to Wembley to see them win the F.A.Cup. In the winter of that year we had the cup in Eastwood which was a 'special event' and finally to close the meeting a group of club officials took the cup to the home of Forest's oldest supporter in Eastwood: Mr. David Hart, and stood it on his living room table.

It is well known what a wonderful record Brian Clough and Peter Taylor had when they were in charge. Promotions were secured from second division to the top division, where the championship was won, and we almost had a season ticket to Wembley to see them win league cups. The final great honour was to win two European Cups in 1979 and 1980. I was lucky enough to get to Munich for the first one.

The records show that in 1856 Barber Walker (the local colliery owners) set aside a plot of land for cricket in Eastwood. Eastwood Amateurs C.C. played on the current Eastwood ground until 1914.

Between the two world wars the club's name was changed to Eastwood Collieries C.C. and in 1922-1924 the local miners, who were keen cricketers built the present pavilion, which has tons of character. I played for the club a few times in the thirties.

During the second world war when cricket ceased there was great deterioration of the ground and for three years after the war football was played on the ground. It was with great help and forsight from Eastwood Town Council that a number of Eastwood cricket lovers were able to re-form the club as Eastwood Town C.C. in 1952 and in the last seventy years the club has gone from strength to strengh. It is sad however that in these days of diversity, it is the only club left in Eastwood. For the past twenty years I have been president of the club, having held all the other positions previously and one of my best memories is when we played Nottinghamshire County C.C. during Tim Robinson's benefit year.

Over the years we have had many fine cricketers playing for the club and easily the best known player was Eastwood's Jeff Astle, who was not only a very fine all- round cricketer, he also scored the winning gaol for West Bromwich Albion at Wembley in a Cup-Final.

The Aim of the Club is to provide entertaining cricket free of charge for the people of Eastwood, and more importantly to encourage the youngsters of the district: Boys and Girls, to play cricket.

I wish all success to the club in the future...

Bill Gregory.

**Mr. & Mrs William (Bill) Gregory in 1959, with the F.A. Cup
Below: F.A. Cup at home of Mr Hart with Eastwood's
Forest Supporters. Photo's by Stan Hutchinson: Eastwood**

EASTWOOD TOWN C.C. N.A.C.L. 1967 'CARRINGTON CUP WINNERS.' BELOW: EASTWOOD CRICKET GROUND & PAVILION: PRE-WORLD WAR TWO.

Harry Riley Book Review
'Coal Mining in the East Midlands'
By David Amos and Natalie Braber
Published by Bradwell Books 2017

The Industrial Revolution and Heritage of the East Midlands would not have been possible without coal mining. For our coal lit the fires of production and kept warm millions of homes throughout the world.
This pictorial record by author's David Amos and Natalie Braber pays striking tribute to the doughty men who risked life and limb daily, by crawling deep underground, often in the most appalling conditions of rat-ridden darkness.

So many collieries, and so many memories are depicted in this worthy volume. Over 100 startling images in superb, glossy, black-and-white photographs.

Like many families, my grandad was a coal-miner in a small Derbyshire village and my own mother once worked in the canteen at Babbington Pit.
Grandad was also a lay-preacher at the local chapel, which his father helped to build. Nearby, Uncle Ben was a miner at Arkright Town, near Chesterfield. So I have an added interest, having grown up around miners and mining.

However, this book is much more than a souvenir of an industry where the last pit in our region closed in 2015, It is a vital educational tool for our young students, lest they forget, all the death, suffering, sweat and toil, their forebears endured to make this country a better, warmer and wealthier place to live.

Opening these pages you will see startling images of men with faces blackened by coal dust, as they dug for black gold. You will read from a former miner, who has devoted his life to promoting the region's mining and cultural heritage and who is a genuine pit-man, through and through, from his safety-lamp to his snap-tin.

Dr. Tony Shaw (Researcher)

Throws a brilliant spotlight on

The D. H. Lawrence Heritage Trail,

Eastwood, Nottinghamshire

including his own very unique 'potted' Biography

'This biography may be slightly unconventional, but that's pure me:

Several years ago I was in the information bureau in Hawera, New Zealand, asking for the exact location of the writer Ronald Hugh Morrieson's grave. The receptionist knew who he was because Morrieson is big in little Hawera (population under 10,000), although I doubt if many people even in New Zealand have heard of him: in his lifetime he only published two (unsuccessful) novels, and then drank himself to death. That sums up my main interests: literature, the obscure, the unusual, and travel. I'm allergic to normality. My books published are **Windmills of Nottinghamshire (1995), Windmilll Wood (1996)** – a biography of the eccentric artist Karl Wood – and **Hidden Nottinghamshire (1998),** a forerunner to my weekly *Nottingham Post* column. We moved from Nottingham to Manchester five years ago, although my partner Penny and I spend about four months a year driving around France chasing up such wonders as the Palais Idéal, a huge oriental-type structure in Hauterives built over many years by a postman collecting pebbles in a wheelbarrow during his long rural round. My writing is now concentrated on my blog, where my MA dissertation on the obscure Nottinghamshire writer James Prior, and my entire PhD on the hopelessly forgotten (and not a little crazy) working-class anarchist writer Lionel Britton, are included.'

Tony Shaw aged 12, with his father on Skegness promenade

Tony in foreground at anti-Thatcher demo

Tony today

Tony shaw: 2018

Tony Shaw:

'I shall cover the D. H. Lawrence Blue Line Trail, published by Broxtowe Borough Council, for most of this post. The blue line is much like the yellow parking restriction lines on roads, only this is on pavements, and stretches from Durban House at the junction of Greenhills Road and Mansfield Road, Eastwood, to The Three Tuns pub on Three Tuns Road.

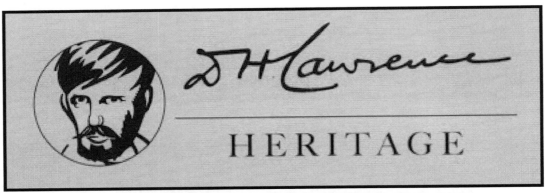

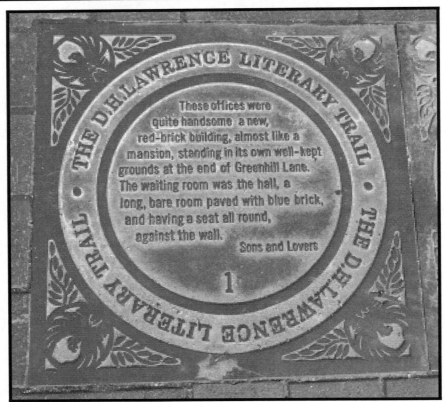

There are fourteen plaques entitled 'The D. H. Lawrence Literary Trail', all of which are gathered outside the square by Eastwood Library, and most of which don't relate to a specific feature of the Blue Line Trail. This one, however, relates to Durban House and as with all the others, contains a quotation by Lawrence:

'These offices were quite handsome: a new, red-brick building, almost like a mansion, standing in its own well-kept grounds at the end of Greenhill Road. The waiting room was a hall, a long, bare room paved with blue brick, and having a seat all round, against the wall.

Sons and Lovers'

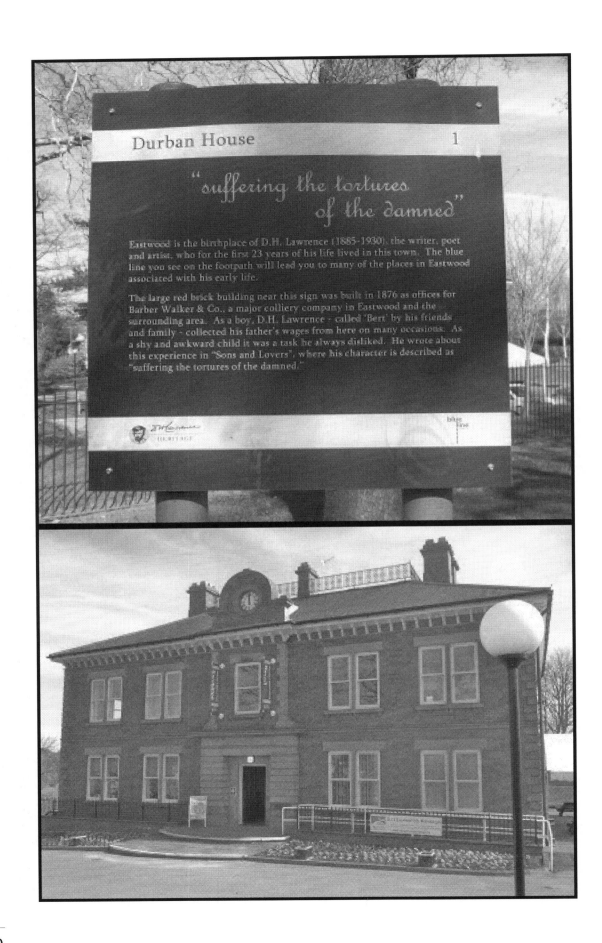

Durban House   1

"suffering the tortures
            of the damned"

Eastwood is the birthplace of D.H. Lawrence (1885-1930), the writer, poet and artist, who for the first 23 years of his life lived in this town. The blue line you see on the footpath will lead you to many of the places in Eastwood associated with his early life.

The large red brick building near this sign was built in 1876 as offices for Barber Walker & Co., a major colliery company in Eastwood and the surrounding area. As a boy, D.H. Lawrence - called 'Bert' by his friends and family - collected his father's wages from here on many occasions. As a shy and awkward child it was a task he always disliked. He wrote about this experience in "Sons and Lovers", where his character is described as "suffering the tortures of the damned."

'Suffering the tortures of the damned'
Barber, Walker & Co. were principal colliery company owners around Eastwood, and this house was built in 1876. Lawrence frequently went there to collect his father's wages, and felt intimidated by the experience. In *Sons and Lovers*, Lawrence fictionalizes life in 'Bestwood' through Paul Morel, and the colliery is owned by Carston, Waite & Co. (H. R. Note: Durban is no longer a Mining and D.H.L. Information Centre, having been sold off to private ownership by Broxtowe Borough Council.

Lawrence's phoenix symbol appears in many places throughout Eastwood. This is one of a number of badges, and is next to the plaque on the pavement outside Durban House.

'Great quadrangles of dwellings on the hillsides'
The colliery company built the houses for the miners to live in, and as Lawrence writes in *Sons and Lovers*, these were large quadrangles. This is Princes Street, a few hundred yards up Mansfield Road from Durban House.

The library was open in two rooms in the Mechanics Hall, on Thursday evenings from 7.0 till 9.0. Paul always fetched the books for his mother, who read a considerable amount, and Miriam trudged down with five or six volumes, for her family. It became the custom for the two to meet in the library.

Sons and Lovers

2

'The library was open in the two rooms in the Mechanics Hall, on Thursday evenings from 7.0 till 9.0. Paul always fetched the books for his mother, who read a considerable amount, and Miriam trudged down with five or six volumes, for her family. It became the custom for the two to meet in the library.

Sons and Lovers'

Miriam Leivers is in part modelled on Lawrences' girlfriend Jessie Chambers of Haggs Farm.

'The outstanding event of the week'

The Mechanics Institute was similar to an adult education college for the working classes, and had a lending library. This would have been one of young Lawrence's outlets to explore literature.

It is now a snooker and pool hall called, ahem, 'Phoenix Cue Sports.
Note the picture of Lawrence next to the function room advert.

'The flat fronted red brick house in Victoria Street'

This is the first house in Eastwood where the Lawrences lived, and where David Herbert Lawrence was born on 11 September 1885, Arthur and Lydia's fourth child.

'I liked our chapel, which was tall and full of light, and yet still; and colourwashed pale green and blue, with a bit of lotus pattern. And over the organ-loft: "O worship the Lord in the beauty of holiness," in big letters.

'Hymns in a Man's Life'

'Three years savage teaching of collier lads'
This plaque is placed at the site of the former Congregational Chapel on
Nottingham Road where the Lawrence family went, and where Lawrence
first met Jessie Chambers. It was demolished in 1971.

Immediately behind the chapel was the British School where Lawrence
went to readings and literary society meetings. And where he
taught between 1902 and 1905, hence the title of the plaque.

An Iceland supermarket is now on the site.

The Breach House   6

" it was a little less common
       to live in the Breach "

This is the house known to all readers of Lawrence as the setting for
"The Bottoms" in "Sons and Lovers". In 1887, the Lawrence family - by
this time seven of them - moved here from Victoria Street and stayed until
1891. Since it was an end house with additional space, they paid an
extra sixpence rent each week. As Lawrence later recalled, "it was a little
less common to live in the Breach."

In "Sons and Lovers" the reader is entertained with much rich information
about Eastwood and the day-to-day life of a mining family. It is within the
fictional setting of this house that we learn of common issues such as the
creative weekly struggle to make ends meet and the strong influence of the
coal mining industry to the area. The kitchen of this house is also the place
where, in the novel, many scenes depicting the often-difficult relationships
within the Lawrence family are played out.

HERITAGE

'It was a little less common to live in the Breach'
Each house move the Lawrences made in Eastwood was to more
superior property. This is in 'The Bottoms' in *Sons and Lovers*,
or the current 28 Garden Road.

'D. H. Lawrence lived here 1887–1891'.

'D. H. LAWRENCE HOUSE

**A MEETING PLACE FOR
THE ARTS, INDUSTRY
AND EDUCATION**

**THE LAWRENCE FAMILY
LIVED HERE
1887–1891'**

'It is finished'
The Lawrences lived here from 1905 to
1911.
This was their only semi-detached house,
and had a garden with a field at the back.
In this house Lydia died in 1910.

'The country of my heart'

Walker Street   10

The Lawrence family lived in this block of six brand new houses from 1891 to 1905, enjoying its elevated position and view across the countryside. It was yet another step up the ladder for the family and the houses were known locally as 'piano row', due to the prosperity of the occupants. The Lawrence's lived in the 'third house', however it is not known from which end of the block to begin counting.

It was in 1901, while the family lived at this house, that his brother Ernest died. The death deeply affected the family, especially Mrs Lawrence, who transferred her hopes and dreams to her youngest son, Bert.

'Bleak House'

The Lawrences lived on Walker Street from 1891–1905, and although this plaque is on number 10, it is uncertain if this is the actual house where they lived: it may be number 8. In 1910 Lawrence's brother Ernest died here. This is a pretty awful shot of the house, but the sun was shining almost directly at the camera.

'Moon and Stars'

This was the name of the Three Tuns in *Sons and Lovers,* which was Lawrence's father's preferred pub, where he would stop off on the way home from Brinsley Colliery. It was also the site of the 'wakes' mentioned in the novel.

Yet another phoenix, this time one of a number on the railings at the junction of Nottingham and Mansfield roads.

In the background of the photo above is this structure, which one website calls the 'D. H. Lawrence Memorial', although the information bureau didn't recognize it by that name. Nevertheless, there is an obvious Lawrence connection, as there's a phoenix on the dome.

Outside Eastwood Library is Neale Andrew's 1989 relief sculpture entitled 'D. H. Lawrence 1885–1930', showing – among other things – a naked couple embracing with miners working underneath, with headstocks and a church in the background.

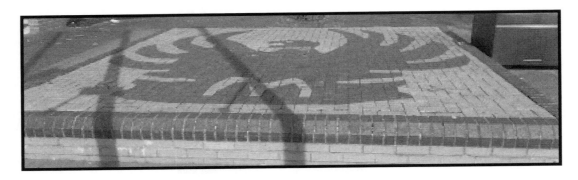

Also in the square by the library – another phoenix.

And in front of the phoenix, the fourteen plaques showing quotations from Lawrence. Three of them have been mentioned already, but here are the remaining eleven:

slope towards Derbyshire and the long slope towards Nottingham.

"Nottingham and the Mining Country"

'They came near to the colliery. It stood quite still and black among the corn-fields, its immense heap of slag seen rising almost from the oats.

"What a pity there is a coal-pit here where it is so pretty," said Clara. "Do you think so?" he answered. "You see I am so used to it I should miss it."

'Mrs Morel loved her marketing. In the tiny market-place on the top of the hill where four roads, from Nottingham and Derby, Ilkeston and Mansfield meet, many stalls were erected.

Sons and Lovers'

'The curtain was down [...] it represented a patchwork of local adverts.
Sons and Lovers'

There was a fat porker and fat pork-pie, and the pig was saying: "You all know where to find me. Inside the crust at Frank Churchill's".

The Lost Girl'

'Paul [...] crept up the stone stairs behind the drapery shop at the Co-op, and peeped into the reading room [...]. Then he looked wistfully out of the window [...]. The valley was full of corn, brightening in the sun.

Sons and Lovers'

'It was a vast square building – vast, that is, for the Woodhouse – standing on the main street and highroad of the small but growing town.

The Lost Girl'

'The wide valley opened out from her, with the far woods withdrawing into twilight, and away in the centre the great pit streaming its white smoke and chuffing as the men were being turned up.

"The Christening"

THE D.H.LAWRENCE LITERARY TRAIL · THE D.H.LAWRENCE LITERARY TRAIL · THE D.H.LAWRENCE LITERARY TRAIL ·

Now Eastwood occupies a lovely position on a hilltop, with the steep slope towards Derbyshire and the long slope towards Nottingham.

'Nottingham and the Mining Country'

10

'Now Eastwood occupies a lovely position on a hilltop, with the steep

'The string of coal-mines of B. W. & Co. had been opened some sixty years before I was born, and Eastwood had come into being as a consequence. It must have been a tiny village at the beginning of the nineteenth century, a small place of cottages...

"Nottingham and the Mining Country"

'I was born nearly forty-four years ago, in Eastwood, a mining village of some three thousand souls, about eight miles from Nottingham, and one mile from the small stream, the Erewash, which divides Nottingham from Derbyshire. It is hilly country...

"Nottingham and the Mining Country"

'The church was away on the left, among black trees. The car slid on downhill, past the Miners Arms. It had already passed the Wellington, the Nelson, the Three Tunns and the Sun [...] and so, past a few new "villas," out into the blackened road between dark hedges and dark-green fields, towards Stack Gate.

Lady Chatterley's Lover'

'To me, it seemed, and still seems, an extremely beautiful countryside, just between the red sandstone and the oak trees of Nottingham, and the cold limestone, the ash trees, the stone fences of Derbyshire.

"Nottingham and the Mining Country".

Other blog posts I've made about D. H. Lawrence are linked below.

D. H. Lawrence in Eastwood, Nottinghamshire

D. H. Lawrence and the University of Nottingham, England

Tony Shaw continues with his blog post: The Breach House: D. H. Lawrence in Eastwood.

'I revisited the birthplace of D. H. Lawrence (1885–1931) in Eastwood earlier this year, although I'd not been to The Breach House before, which is now 28 Garden Road. The Lawrence family moved here in 1887 from 8a Victoria Street, and as it was an end terrace house it was an improvement; it also had a porch (just visible in shadow on the left here), a small scullery, and most important of all a relatively large garden. It belonged to the colliery owners the miner Arthur worked for, and cost sixpence (2½ pence) more a week to rent than their former home. David Herbert was two years old, and the rest of the family consisted of his parents Lydia and Arthur, his elder brothers Ernest and George, his elder sister Emily and his younger sister Ada.

To some, this is known as the '*Sons and Lovers*' house because of Lawrence's representation of it in his novel of 1913. This area Lawrence fictionally referred to as 'The Bottoms': the house faces a slope, and the children used to play there.

The front, south-facing room was known as the 'parlour' and was only used on Sundays and special occasions.

The kitchen also served as the living room.

Through the kitchen door is the scullery, with the shelves of the pantry (or larder) opposite.

'Outside is the water pump on the left. I'm unsure if this would have been used by the Lawrences then: they may have had tap water from the scullery as shown above – I'm not too strong on the history of water supply. On the right is a device for heating water.'

The rusty bracket of the pig hook.

The spacious garden, where it certainly can't always have been idyllic:

'Lawrence's fictionalized description of living in the house in *Sons and Lovers* is probably very similar to how he and his family experienced The Breach House:

'The dwelling-room, the kitchen, was at the back of the house, facing inward between the blocks, looking at a scrubby back garden, and then at the ash-pits. And between the rows, between the long lines of ash-pits, went the alley, where the children played and the women gossiped and the men smoked. So, the actual conditions of living in the Bottoms, that was so well built and that looked so nice, were quite unsavoury because people must live in the kitchen, and the kitchens opened on to that nasty alley of ash-pits."

'The ash-pits were emptied regularly by the night soil workers, but the smell if the wind was blowing towards the south, particularly on a hot day, must have been scarcely tolerable. (The lavatory was on the left of the photo, with a small area for coal storage on the right.) In 1891 the Lawrences moved to better accommodation: a brand new rented house on Walker Street, which didn't belong to the colliery company.'

Note: We greatly appreciated the opportunity The D. H. Lawrence Society provided, through Heritage Open Days, to see The Breach House, Lawrence's other museum in Eastwood. The house is not normally open to the general public, and the two upper floors may now provide holiday accommodation.

❖❖❖

Tony Shaw website:

http://tonyshaw3.blogspot.co.uk/2012/09/the-breach-house-d-h-lawrence-in.html

Part Three

Owd Allam Fails

By Danny Corns

'**Hallam Fields and Stanton Ironworks** have to be talked about in the same breath.

Hallam fields would not have existed without Stanton and I believe Stanton needed the Hallam Field type of person to become the great industry it eventually became.

Perhaps I could clarify this statement:

In the middle of the 18th century Abraham Darby of Coalbrook Dale, Shropshire, perfected the use of coke for blast furnace work. This replaced charcoal and in a very short time 70% of iron in this country was made with coke as the fuel. This practice spread rapidly to Staff., and this county became the leading iron making area in England. This meant that Staff., and Shropshire men became the iron making experts.

According to 'Glovers History of Derbyshire,' in our county the principle sources of iron stone were at Codnor Park, Morley, Somercotes, Chesterfield and Stavely, with a small deposit near Dale Abbey. A small furnace was built in 1788 at what is now known as Furnace Pond. It lasted less than 15 years.

A considerable interval occured between the blowing out of the Dale furnace and the commencement of the building of the three old works furnaces in 1845.

On 27th April 1846 Benjamin Smith and his son Josiah, trading as Smith & Son, were granted a lease by Earl Stanhope, of ironsone coal and fireclay in the Parishes of Dale and Stanton-by-Dale . It became The Stanton Iron Company.

In 1849, when, after the Smiths had financial difficulties, James Hayward, a mortgagee, obtained a foreclosure order in respect of his security in 1855. He eventually became bankrupt and George Crompton, Newton and Co., were allowed to bid. They obtained possession for £16,000, exclusive of rolling stock which was agreed to be at £7,200.

No:1 furnace was erected in 1865 and No:5 furnace about 1867. With five furnaces in full blast and with plans to extend the works with more furnaces and foundries, it was obvious that more specialised labour was required.

The Franco-Prussion War of 1870 created a tremendous boom in the iron and coal trades. Prices were forced up and very large profits were made. The prospect induced the building of many new furnaces, including the Stanton New works in the early 1870's.

In 1868 there were only 24 cottages (North View) and Job Severns farm at Hallam Fields. It was known at that time as New England and By some as Mountain Ash. Where the New Works stood was meadow land with a brook running, and fish to be caught. The Romans knew the area and it was possibly a settlement site from Saxon Times, witness the word: 'Brendiche'-meaning Burnt land. Why clear land if not for use? Maybe for agricultural purposes.

The whole of the present Hallam Fields was the 'Bindage Meadow'.

Early landowners were the Cantelupes, Savages, and Manners. Later in C18 it was divided between the Manners, Flamstead, Hudson, Leeper, Kirkby, England and Taylor families.

Crompton Street (top end) was built contemporary with the New Works: known locally as 'Knockers Row' or Gawp Street, why? When strangers were about the knocks started from the top house downwards, then people came out to gawp!In the early 1870's locals were called to service at No.9 North View by the Rev. Alfred Newdigate ringing a hand bell. The Rev. E. Evens of Kirk Hallam had Job Severn's barn fitted out as a mission church in 1876. This doubled as a day-school during the week until the building of the 'Iron Church' in 1880, in memory of Gilbert-Deborah-Crompton, with the Rev. G. Oliver in charge.

Cinder Row and the 9 cottages at South View had been built. The Railway Inn, later Mitchell's grocery shop, was the local. Post office Row (Frog Row), The rRifle Range and bottom end of Crompton Street appeared just after.

The church of St. Bartholomew erected in 1896, at a cost of £3,500 completes the iron-making settlement, almost ostracized from Ilkeston.

On the first day of the coming of the tram in 1903, 20,000 curious people travelled to and from Hallam fields, surprised I expect to find no mud huts.

On Crompton Street the Clock Tower was erected in 1905 with 4 bells and in 1911 a chiming apparatus and 4 more bells were added.

The arrival in 1908 of the Rev. M. Cox marked the beginning of an era. His influence on the populace over the next 40 years was enormous. He formed the Church Lads Brigade (CLB.) known as Cox's Little Boggers.

As Stanton's first welfare officer, most of the lads' careers were formed by him, in fact I believe Hallam Fields people owe Parson-Cox a great debt.

Copee's horse drawn brake was used for outings and by football teams.

'We're goo-in to Nanpantom,

Where they dunna want 'em.'

This was chanted on-route to Charnwood Forest.

The Night-soil men had to contend with kids yawping.

'The corporation shit-cart was full up to the brim,

The driver fell in backwards and said he couldn't swim.'

Kids learned to swim in delightful parts of the Bottom Cut, known as 'ot waters,' 'tar-side,' 'sandy bottoms,' 'packy,' and 'war-ole.'

Competition was intense among the local 'tater growers.' they started off even, with one pound of three different types of seed potato each. When weighing took place during october, if the judges weren't looking, some competitors were not averse to slipping heavier spuds on to his weighing tray.

On Jan 31st 1916 the Zeppolin LZ 2D flattened the parish room and tram sheds. A number of inhabitants at the top end of 'gawp street' needed to change their trousers as a result.

Coughing kids were held over hot, tar-filled dipping tanks at Stanton.

'Sowjers field,' 'Isan-ills,' 'Coke-heath,' 'Big-tip.' All marvelous names-'Teasin-the tecs,' 'The dens we made. All gone, never to return.

The school motto, I believe, epitomised it's people:

'Whoever you are, be noble

Whaever you do, do well

Whenever you speak, speak kindly

And give joy, where-ever you dwell'

Women came in to deliver babies and sit all night in times of illness.

Double figure families were common. The essense of Hallam Fields people was quality and kindness.

Less than 100 years old at the start of destruction in 1962, it came, it went and 'Ilson' hardly knew it existed.'

Broxtowe Borough Partnership

NHS
Nottingham West
Clinical Commissioning Group

Eastwood Memory Cafe

We meet on the 2nd Tuesday of every month from 12.30 - 3pm at Plumptre Hall behind St Mary's Church Church Street Eastwood Nottingham NG16 3BS

Eastwood Memory Cafe runs on a monthly basis for people diagnosed with dementia and those who care and support them. There is a £1 charge for each person attending the cafe (though no charge for Care and Nursing Home staff). All money raised is invested back into Eastwood Memory Cafe. A carer or supporter must accompany the person affected by dementia to the cafe as we are unable to offer respite care.

The venue is located in central Eastwood and is disabled friendly with good access and available parking. It is on a bus route for those who do not drive. Eastwood Cars are very kindly giving a discount to our guests, please phone 01773 770000 or 01773 768009 and quote "Eastwood Memory Cafe".

We aim to provide:

- **The opportunity for people with dementia, their carers and volunteers to have lunch together and for all to socialise**

- **A safe space to talk without fear of being judged**

- **An encouraging and safe environment**

- **Stimulating mental and physical activities**

- **Therapeutic treatments for relaxation**

- **Support**

- **Signposting to local services**

- **Trips and visits out to further engage with the wider community and enhance well-being and happiness**

- **Opportunities and support for a more dementia friendly community**

If you are interested in attending Eastwood Memory Cafe then please contact Medical Centre c/o Diane Rowley or email your enquiry to eastwoodmemorycafe@btinternet.com

Above Pics show Eastwood Memory Cafe 'Open Day and Cheque Presentation' at Eastwood Town Council Chambers, by Notts. County Councillor Tony Harper to Diane Rowley in the presence of Eastwood Town Mayor: David Townes.

Accommodation Report

Wellington Court

Wellington Place, Eastwood, Nottingham, Notts, NG16 3GQ.
View on a map

Manager: Anchor, 2 Godwin Street, Bradford, Yorkshire BD1 2ST
Telephone: 0800 251 1609
Email: contact@anchor.org.uk
Web: http://www.anchor.org.uk.
Developer: Anchor, http://www.anchor.org.uk.

Manager:

Developer:

Update
- Update info
- Add vacancies

Type(s):	Retirement housing.
Properties:	35 flats. Built in 1984. Sizes 1 bedroom. Includes wheelchair standard properties.
Services:	Resident management staff and Careline alarm service.
Facilities:	Lift, lounge, laundry, guest facilities, garden, hobby room, activities room.
Lifestyle:	Social activities are actively encouraged. New residents accepted from 55 years of age. Both cats & dogs generally accepted (subject to conditions).
Tenure:	Tenure(s): Rent (social landlord).
Manager's notes:	At Wellington Court sheltered housing scheme in Eastwood, we offer purpose-built properties for rent for people over the age of 55. You can enjoy your retirement and get the best out of life in comfortable surroundings with the benefit of having a scheme manager and a 24-hour alarm service if ever you have an emergency. You will not need to worry about maintenance and repairs as we take care of those. We provide a wide range of facilities, including a communal lounge, a garden or outside seating area, an on-site laundry, parking bays and, in many schemes, a guest room for visitors. Sometimes you may want to be on your own and other times you may want to be sociable. Our properties give you that freedom and our scheme manager can help arrange social activities where you can meet other like-minded people. We know pets are important to some people and we have a policy which welcomes small pets. If you want to know more, please get in touch.
Info updated:	04/06/2011.

Properties available

Check with Manager above - none notified to EAC.

EAC A leader in information and advice to older people

Open Day at Wellington Court Eastwood : Pics by Harry Riley, during his joint visit with Brian Fretwell.

Local review

2017 Tour of Britain Cycle Race

3rd to 10th Sept.

Riders competing 117 miles over 8 days across the UK

(Mansfield Starting Stage and passing through Eastwood Notts.)

'Hilltop and Greasley Parish do them proud.'

Wed. 6th Sept, and the crowds turned out, families, men, women and invalids on powered scooters, and local schoolchildren and their teachers lining the route. many armed with Union Flags.

Expectation was high and although the weather was looking anything but bright, the rainclouds threatened and held off.

'Storm Gods' could only manage an odd spit-and-spurtle, not enough to dampen our enthusiasm for this very special event.

Towards mid–day police motorcycle outriders began to appear, with hooters sounding and blue lights a-flashing. These were quickly followed up by the leading entourage of Team-cars with support bikes mounted on roof bars high above, and then a megaphone truck-hailing: **'Here they come, Look out for the Rider wearing the Green Jersey!'**

The Course-Marshalls did their best, but still cars and commercial vehicles had persisted in trying to ruin our parade by circumventing the road-closure bollards, and had to be turned back, by local police, to loud applause from the waiting public.

Camera's, were clicking away for all they were worth, amongst the yells and screams of encouragement, as the main bunch of cyclists (The Peloton) came into view.

The public reception, so far, throughout this inspiring race has been fit for a queen, and the press and television coverage superb. So many small towns and parishes have worked wonders to get behind this National Event with brightly painted bikes ,balloons and bunting and the barmiest-crack-pot inventions, such as monkeys-on bikes, bikes up trees, dummy cyclists stuck in hedges etc. etc.

To paraphrase that famous 'St. Crispin's day speech' fom Shakespeare's Henry V- Men now abed will think themselves accursed they were not here!'

Chapter and Verse footnote: Young children from the nearby Eastwood Priory Catholic Voluntary Academy were present with their teachers at Hilltop, armed with huge smiles and their colourful Union Flags, and so clearly enjoying the moment, that we thought to approach their teachers and suggest a small competition which we would judge, with awards for Prose and Poetry-for the two winners and the two runners up. This was accepted and at the end of February half-term 2018 Broxtowe and Eastwood Councillors: David and Susan Bagshaw presented additional prizes from their own pockets. **'A great day to remember.'**

We hope the next big cycle race to pass through our area on 8th September 2018 will be equally well recieved. It is surely events like this which stick in the mind and are long remembered, coming back into sharp focus as we grow older and which help to shape the knowledge and respect of future generations.

From personal experience, a first adult pedal bike was the first real love of my life, it gave me the freedom to roam far and wide, exploring the country lanes of Notts and Derbyshire and to dream of one day owning a Dawes Debonair or a really lightweight racing bike. I drooled over cycle catalogues and pics of top riders with bikes such as the Raleigh Record Ace, and thinking, perhaps one day...

2017 Tour of Britain Cycle Race approaching Hilltop, Eastwood Notts. Wed 6th Sept. Peloton just visible in the distance.

And here comes the main body of riders.

Priory Award Winners with 'Claire-Presentation Teacher' and Eastwood and Broxtowe Councillors David and Susan Bagshaw

2017 saw the 200th Anniversary of the Pentrich Revolution. This important date was commemorated throughout Notts and Derbyshire:

with events taking place in towns and villages along the route of the ill-fated march.

Local libraries featured photographic displays and several out of print books on the subject were re-issued, including new ones. The Pentrich and South Wingfield Revolution Group received a grant from the National Lottery towards the cost of the awareness campaign and walks were staged, including a walk from Pentrich to Giltbrook stopping at key points along the way. I joined the major walk at Eastwood's Sun Inn checkpoint and we made another stop at Eastwood Library, then the walkers continued to Giltbrook. With the technical help of Charlie Brown of Kingsmill Hospital's Millside Radio We recorded a conversational poem for Youtube. This is a dramatised, fictional account, based on the facts concerning Jeremiah Brandtreth's last days in Derby Gaol, prior to his execution. It is called The 'Starving Scarecrow Soldiers' and is taken from my poetry volume 'Rhyme and a little Reason' published by Amazon books.

Link to audio: www.youtube.com/watch?v=#A648D8

My other books concerning the Pentrich Revolution:

'Butchered and Bled for a Loaf o' Bread'

'Twisting in and other strange tales'

The Pentrich Revolution Bicentenary

Claiming our place in *History*

"Every man his skill must try;
He must stand up and not deny;
No bloody soldier must he dread,
He must turn out and fight for bread;
For the time has come you plainly see,
The government opposed must be." (Jeremiah Brandreth 1817)

"For a parliamentary Reform....on the principles of what is called
Universal Suffrage." (Thomas Bacon 1817)

heritage
lottery fund
LOTTERY FUNDED

CAROLINE SALLOWAY – MUSIC TEACHER,

SPRINGBANK PRIMARY SCHOOL, EASTWOOD

Caroline Salloway (nee Dilnot) is a pianist, singer/songwriter and worship leader. She has been involved in music for over 25 years. Her life's passion is to help develop and inspire others with a passion for music whatever standard they are at. It's never too late to learn a new skill and music is no exception to the rule. Caroline currently works at Springbank Primary School, Eastwood, Nottingham, helping the next generation to develop their musical skills and is also a worship leader at New Horizon Church Assemblies of God Church in Eastwood, Nottingham, where her brother, Andy Dilnot, is the Senior Pastor.

Caroline was born in the 70s in Northampton but moved to Nottingham when she was just a baby. Caroline's mother, who's from Mansfield, was also a singer, played the piano and was an accomplished dancer (dancing with the likes of Cliff Richard and Tommy Steele). It was her mother that inspired her with her piano playing at the age of 9. Her Mum used to play tunes on the family piano that was bought for her by her father in the 1950's. Caroline couldn't stop listening to her Mum and would not let her go until she showed her how to play too! Her mother and father both loved music; often listening to the sounds of Abba, James Last and Frank Sinatra, as well as having a love for the musicals and rock & roll. Caroline recalls her parents taking her to see the musical 'The Sound of Music' in London where she remembers feeling moved to tears by the musical score. When her parents realised her love for music, Caroline started piano lessons at the age of 10 years old. She continued with piano lessons, including passing her London College of Music Pianoforte Examinations up until the age of 17.

From a young age, Caroline would sing and play the piano in front of people at events, church or family dos. From around the age of 14, she developed her gift of the piano, whilst attending the Church Youth Group, where she would play during the worship sets and learned to play in the band and sing. Caroline went on to lead the Church Worship Team from 1996 to 2006, until she had her first child. During this time Caroline also led many musical events and composed songs. Caroline was married in 1996 to Derby born, Simon Salloway. Simon is an accomplished self-taught Sound Engineer so it goes without saying that they make a good team. Simon has helped Caroline co-produce most of her recorded songs to date.

Caroline has lived in the Nottingham area nearly all her life and because of her church links with the town of Eastwood and her working history, she has always been very much involved in the community. After leaving college at 18, with a Business Studies qualification, Caroline worked in the offices for British Coal in Eastwood and then Microlise, Farrington Way, Eastwood for 12 years, where she worked in Sales and Marketing. Until very recently, she also worked in the New Horizon Church office, also based in Eastwood helping the church with their admin, events and assemblies. In 2012 she visited Springbank Primary School on several occasions to take some assemblies where she played the piano and sang to the children, after subsequent visits, she was then offered a job there as a Music Tutor.

Working with primary school children continues to be an absolute pleasure, where she provides piano, recorder and singing lessons, but really is passionate about all aspects of music. She has a vast experience of music in and out of school and loves to see children flourish in their musical skills. As well as her music qualifications, she also has a Teaching Assistant Level 3 certificate.

Caroline is still a worship leader to date at New Horizon AOG Church, Eastwood. She is also very passionate about bringing change to the local area through the church and community working together; helping with poverty and those in need, through local Uniform Banks, Food banks and working with other charities that can help those in need. Caroline organises the annual musical Community Carol Concert at New Horizon Church and the offering taken is always given to a chosen charity. Lastly, in 2017, Caroline produced a Charity Christmas single with Springbank Primary School 'All Around the World it's Christmas Time'. It was aired on UCB (United Christian Broadcasters) radio and the story was covered in the local papers. She plans to

continue writing and producing songs now and into the future for school and church to raise money for charitable causes.

Caroline's dream is that many children continue their passion for music into adulthood so that the art of performing and piano playing can live on.

Every Sunday morning New Horizon Church hold a Church Service for all the community to attend and enjoy at Eastwood Hall Park Academy, Mansfield Rd, NG16 3EA at 11 am. Join us from 10.15 am to relax before our service starts and grab yourself a coffee, tea and cake. It's a space to meet friends, make friends and connect with each other in a warm, friendly and welcoming atmosphere. The service includes modern and contemporary worship accompanied with relevant and inspiring teaching from the Bible, as well as providing a free kids' programme. For more info visit our website www.newhorizonchurch.org.uk. Everyone welcome.

'Ben of Bennerley'
by Harry Riley

I'm sure **'The Friends of Bennerley Viaduct'** can tell you all you've ever wished to know about this magnificent, 60 foot high, ancient feat of sound British engineering, and which is now devoid of its railway tracks, it's supporting brick columns and access footbridge. So what can an old dodger like me add to the story of it's illustrious past and it's promising future, as the priceless gem in a possible World-Heritage Nature Reserve-underscored by **rare plants** and even rarer-mini-wildlife (Frogs and **Great Crested Newts.**)

There are some great pics of the Viaduct from above and below on the Internet, but I firmly believed the best way to study this grade-two-listed structure was to see for it for myself, up close and personal. So after much soul-searching, I decided to undertake an inspiring pilgimage, as befitted an aged grandfather, 'long past his Biblical sell-by-date of three score and ten years' and with noisy-became slippy and dangerously wet. Luckily, on the ground, covered in moss, I found the very aid, a firm and trusty stave, which eventually, after much hardship, and cracking knees.

So, on a bright day, the nearer I scrambled, the darker and more dificult it became, you see I wished to view the structure from above, and from the end of the viaduct which has long since had it's fragile, safety-access-steps removed, I imagine, to avoid wild young teenagers and reckless, 'coffin-dodging' pensioners undertaking stupid risks. This high-Kimberley-end of the viaduct is now lost amongst the clouds and peaks of densely packed woodland brambles and trees.

Ignoring dire warnings **'To Please be Careful'** from a considerate lady 'flora-and-forna' hunter, way down below. I stumbled, slipping and sliding, and proceeded blithely on my quest.

The higher I got though, it soon became clear, even to my fossilized brain, that what I really needed was a sturdy pole for support, as the steep, pathless, gradient gritting of false teeth, enabled me to achieve my intended goal.

Without it I could never have conquered my chosen 'Everest.'

Standing triumphant at the top I ventured onto the spaced out cross-girders and cautiously bestrode them towards the middle. Glancing down I saw a group of walkers gazing up at me, They seemed perplexed, and it suddenly dawned on me that they may have thought I was a **'jumper'** and were anticipating a little extra excitement. If that were so, I have to apologize, for I took a much slower way down and lived to tell the tale.

Back home I cleaned the stave, stained, and fitted it with the steel-shank of a sprained 'Bulldog' garden fork, before naming (with heated poker-art) my new friend; this stripling-son-of-the-soil- **'Ben of Bennerly.'**(final 'e' missing, to add to it's rustic individuality).

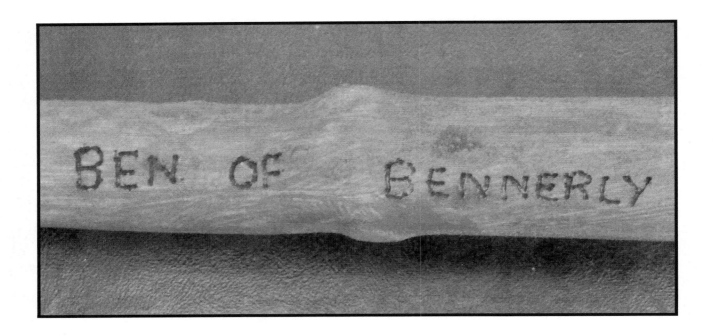

Bennerley 'Listed' Viaduct

Bennerley Viaduct viewed from above

Sheared off bolt discovered at the base of Bennerley Viaduct. Nov. 2017. How many more have broken away or are likely to do so, before we lose this priceless listed structure.

Bennerley Viaduct

About the Project

1. We aim to **Restore Bennerley Viaduct** and bring it back into use as a walking and cycling trail. This will give the viaduct a new purpose.

2. We will **inform, explain and celebrate** the achievements of our Victorian engineers and share our admiration of this magnificent wrought iron structure.

3. We will ensure that the **lifespan of Bennerley Viaduct is extended** so future generations can enjoy it.

4. We will **connect** the viaduct to the area's trail network. The viaduct will become the centrepiece of the developing Great Northern Greenway **connecting** both arms of the Erewash Valley Trail.

5. We will **improve access** around, on and underneath the viaduct so this iconic structure can be fully appreciated.

6. We will **enhance the natural heritage** of the viaduct area and manage the land to increase biodiversity

7. We hope to **improve the health of the local community** by providing opportunities to walk and cycle in the outdoors.

8. We will **promote the literary heritage** and the connections between the area and D.H. Lawrence.

9. We will involve local schools, colleges and young people and **developing educational and training opportunities** using the viaduct as a focus.

10. We will **develop people's skills** to improve employment prospects. (Heritage restoration skills and wildlife/ecological skills.)

THE FRIENDS OF BENNERLEY VIADUCT

For further information:
Web: www.bennerleyviaduct.org
Facebook: Friends of Bennerley Viaduct
Phone: Sustrans 0115 853 2953
Email: MidlandsandEast@sustrans.org.uk

sustrans
JOIN THE MOVEMENT

Owd Allam Fails

By Danny Corns

Hallam Fields and Stanton Ironworks have to be talked about in the same breath.

Hallam fields would not have existed without Stanton and I believe Stanton needed the Hallam Field type of person to become the great industry it eventually became.

Perhaps I could clarify this statement:

In the middle of the 18th century Abraham Darby of Coalbrook Dale, Shropshire, perfected the use of coke for blast furnace work. This replaced charcoal and in a very short time 70% of iron in this country was made with coke as the fuel. This practice spread rapidly to Staffordshire and this county became the leading iron making area in England. This meant that Staffordshire and Shropshire men became the iron making experts.

According to 'Glovers History of Derbyshire,' in our county the principal sources of iron stone were at Codnor Park, Morley, Somercotes, Chesterfield and Stavely, with a small deposit near Dale Abbey. A small furnace was built in 1788 at what is now known as Furnace Pond. It lasted less than 15 years.

A considerable interval occurred between the blowing out of the Dale furnace and the commencement of the building of the three old works furnaces in 1845.

On 27th April 1846 Benjamin Smith and his son Josiah, trading as Smith & Son, were granted a lease by Earl Stanhope, of ironstone coal and fireclay in the Parishes of Dale and Stanton-by-Dale . It became The Stanton Iron Company.

In 1849, when, after the Smiths had financial difficulties, James Hayward, a mortgagee, obtained a foreclosure order in respect of his security in 1855. He eventually became bankrupt and George Crompton, Newton and Co. were allowed to bid. They obtained possession for £16,000, exclusive of rolling stock which was agreed to be at £7,200.

No:1 furnace was erected in 1865 and No:5 furnace about 1867. With five furnaces in full blast and with plans to extend the works with more furnaces and foundries, it was obvious that more specialised labour was required.

The Franco-Prussion War of 1870 created a tremendous boom in the iron and coal trades. Prices were forced up and very large profits were made. The prospect induced the building of many new furnaces, including the Stanton New works in the early 1870's.

In 1868 there were only 24 cottages (North View) and Job Severns farm at Hallam Fields. It was known at that time as New England and By some as Mountain Ash. Where the New Works stood was meadow land with a brook running, and fish to be caught. The Romans knew the area and it was possibly a settlement site from Saxon Times, witness the word: 'Brendiche'-meaning Burnt land. Why clear land if not for use? Maybe for agricultural purposes.

The whole of the present Hallam Fields was the 'Bindage Meadow'.

Early landowners were the Cantelupes, Savages, and Manners. Later in the eighteenth century it was divided between the Manners, Flamstead, Hudson, Leeper, Kirkby, England and Taylor families.

Crompton Street (top end) was built contemporary with the New Works: known locally as 'Knockers Row' or Gawp Street. Why? When strangers were about the knocks started from the top house downwards, then people came out to gawp! In the early 1870's locals were called to service at No.9 North View by the Rev. Alfred Newdigate ringing a hand bell. The Rev. E. Evens of Kirk Hallam had Job Severn's barn fitted out as a mission church in 1876. This doubled as a day-school during the week until the building of the 'Iron Church' in 1880, in memory of Gilbert-Deborah-Crompton, with the Rev. G. Oliver in charge.

Cinder Row and the 9 cottages at South View had been built. The Railway Inn, later Mitchell's grocery shop, was the local. Post office Row (Frog Row), The Rifle Range and bottom end of Crompton Street appeared just after.

The church of St. Bartholomew erected in 1896, at a cost of £3,500 completes the iron-making settlement, almost ostracized from Ilkeston.

On the first day of the coming of the tram in 1903, 20,000 curious people travelled to and from Hallam fields, surprised I expect to find no mud huts.

On Crompton Street the Clock Tower was erected in 1905 with 4 bells and in 1911 a chiming apparatus and 4 more bells were added.

The arrival in 1908 of the Rev. M. Cox marked the beginning of an era. His influence on the populace over the next 40 years was enormous. He formed the Church Lads Brigade (CLB.) known as Cox's Little Boggers.

As Stanton's first welfare officer, most of the lads' careers were formed by him, in fact I believe Hallam Fields people owe Parson-Cox a great debt.

Cope's horse drawn brake was used for outings and by football teams.

'We're goo-in to Nanpantom,

Where they dunna want 'em.'

This was chanted en route to Charnwood Forest.

The Night-soil men had to contend with kids yawping.

'The corporation shit-cart was full up to the brim,

The driver fell in backwards and said he couldn't swim.'

Kids learned to swim in delightful parts of the Bottom Cut, known as 'ot waters,' 'tar-side,' 'sandy bottoms,' 'packy,' and 'war-ole.'

Competition was intense among the local 'tater growers.' they started off even, with one pound of three different types of seed potato each. When weighing took place during october, if the judges weren't looking, some competitors were not averse to slipping heavier spuds on to his weighing tray.

On Jan 31st 1916 the Zeppelin L 20 flattened the parish room and tram sheds. A number of inhabitants at the top end of 'gawp street' needed to change their trousers as a result.

Coughing kids were held over hot, tar-filled dipping tanks at Stanton.

'Sowjers field,' 'Isan-ills,' 'Coke-heath,' 'Big-tip.' All marvelous names-'Teasin-the tecs,' 'The dens we made. All gone, never to return.

The school motto, I believe, epitomised it's people:

'Whoever you are, be noble

Whatever you do, do well

Whenever you speak, speak kindly

And give joy, where-ever you dwell'

Women came in to deliver babies and sit all night in times of illness.

Double figure families were common. The essense of Hallam Fields people was quality and kindness.

Less than 100 years old at the start of destruction in 1962, it came, it went and 'Ilson' hardly knew it existed.

Danny's family biography

The Corns family arrived at Hallam Fields in the late 1890's having moved from Riddings to follow the Iron Trade . Grandad Albert was born in Tipton, Staffs, (which was then the centre of the Iron Trade). Albert lost his wife (Kate Townsend) soon after arriving, leaving Grandad to raise three sons. He met Grandma, Marian Eliza Randall, then a widow with one son Noel.

In those days kids needed both a Mam and Dad. The husband was the breadwinner, with the wife bringing up the kids. They went on to have eight more kids, making 14 people living in a two-bedroomed house with a small box-room, parlour, living room and scullery. The midden was at the end of the yard. This was not unusual in those days. Most Hallam Fields families arrived from the 'Black Country,' Tipton, Dudley, Bilston, and surrounding Iron-making areas, on barges along the Grand Union and Erewash Canals, with their families and furniture, ready to occupy the new houses recently built on Crompton Street.

These iron-making experts arrived as a result of the 1870 Franco-Prussian War, when the New Works was built, especially to provide Iron to both sides. My family were 'moulders' in the main, with most of the men working for at least 52 years for the Stanton Company.

I served my apprenticeship there as an engineering fitter. We left Crompton Street in 1952 to occupy one of the new houses just built by the company in Kirk Hallam. How times change!

Danny Corns

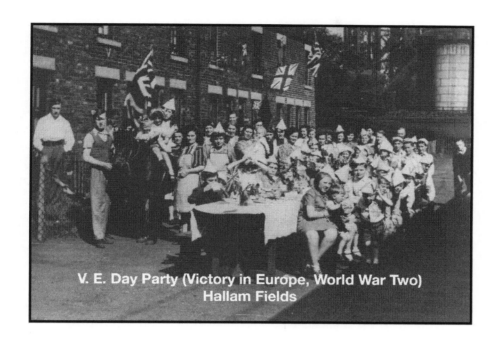

V. E. Day Party (Victory in Europe, World War Two)
Hallam Fields

Grocers Shop, Crompton Street, Hallam Fields

Crompton Street Hallam Fields showing Hotel

'Copes Hearse' (Ref: Danny Corns Hallam Fields)

❖❖❖

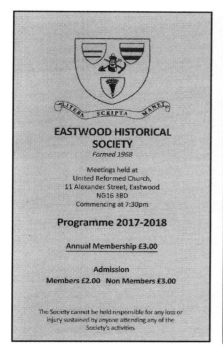

❖❖❖

Old Ilkeston

http://www.oldilkeston.co.uk/dalby-house-and-dr-norman/

Early/mid-Victorian Ilkeston and its people.

Dalby House and Dr. Norman

Dalby House

Deriving its name from owner John Dalby in 1806, **Dalby House** elicited a not altogether complimentary description from local historian, Venerable Whitehead, writing in the Pioneer of 1854. He complained that Dalby House had an *"economy of space on its ground floor"* more suitable to a house on the crowded streets of London than the abode of a country gentleman. However its site was fit for a castle and afforded magnificent views over the meandering Erewash river, over the villages of Cossall and Strelley, and over the hills of Bramcote.

In the same article **the Park** is described as a *"picturesque residence – but its modern Gothic is not the perfection of domestic architecture"*. Venerable Whitehead continued: *"We love its ivy covered walls and its bowery trees – its English comfort and English hospitality; and the noble specimen of an Englishman presented in the person of its honoured occupant – the chief of his clan"*.

That chief would be coal master Samuel Potter, the occupant of the Park.

Apart from a labourer's cottage the only residence other than the Park in that immediate neighbourhood was **the Larklands house**.

In 1881 this was described as *"of peculiar formation, consisting of a number of rooms opening into a long passage. The doors of these rooms being locked on the outside, it is not possible to proceed from one to the other, so that the only mode of entrance (is) by the (sash) windows"*. (NG)

From the lofty Market Place the Ilkeston News (1855) waxed lyrical about the view over the *"broad and ample scenery of the valley of the Erewash and the dale of Stanton. "Rich woods greet the eye, — here and there covering the summits, in the summer season displaying bright green splendours, tinged with the delicate hues of the rainbow. We do not know a more cheering ride than a few miles to, and a little way beyond, the romantic village of Trowell, whose time-worn tower awakens endearing associations of long past days. The country near the old bridge at 'Gallows Inn', (ominous name) is truly of a superior character, — the river winds its silent way through rich meadow land, and as the hill rises on the Nottinghamshire side it is right well greeted by the far stretching ascent opposite, on which the Ilkeston church appears with conspicuous front, commanding the scenery around for many miles".*

Old Park or Old Hollows

At Dalby House we can contemplate a letter to the Pioneer of June 1866, signed by *'Ilkestonian'* and bemoaning the lack of a 'People's Park' in the town, *"where the men, women, and children ... can walk and play".*

The Cricket Ground was not a pleasant nor safe place, and was only available by courtesy of the cricketers. *Ilkestonian's* own solution lay in the field called the *'Old Park'*, part of Church property, east of the Vicarage, which on Sunday afternoons is *'literally thronged'*.

'Ilkestonian' described it thus:

"Its sunny banks and enticing slopes seeming to possess a real charm for the various young people who desire to luxuriously bask themselves in the warm sunshine, or run down the mimic hills; and last Sunday afternoon the sight of 70 or 100 congregated there made me wish we could...procure this pleasant place for a perpetual and rightful Park for our townspeople. The land is so overrun by children, and so intersected by footpaths, that it cannot be very profitable to the occupier; moreover it possesses such pleasing variety of surface that half the usual labour necessary for forming a recreation ground would be done away with. It would require only the walks forming, shrubs planting, and a lodge building".

Taking an early evening walk in this same field, just prior to Christmas of the following year, a correspondent in the same newspaper encountered two drunken would-be pugilists. They were obviously intent upon doing serious harm to each other and the correspondent listened intently to their 'unintelligent stultilogence'.

"Thae wants to feight mae, dustner?

Ah!

Well, pool off thee coot and feight.

Nay, ah shonner; ahl feight thae weight on.

Nay, poolt off.

Well, hit mae.

Ah wool.

Well, dowt; thae dahner

Ah dah.

The fight then began in earnest as the two engaged in a horizontal wrestling match at ground level, the taller and stronger of the pair eventually wrapping his hands around the windpipe of the other. At this point the observer cried out.

"My good man, come away from that worthless fellow, and don't take the trouble to hurt him".

His interjection was sufficient.

The fighters retreated and he was left to contemplate the nature of the town's social problems:

"What a shame and pity it is that education and temperance do not more effectually and extensively prevail over the manners and habits of the lower classes of Ilkeston!"

Fifteen years later and *'Rambler'*, writing in the Pioneer, was still pleading for this area – familiarly known as the Old Hollows – to be developed as a place of recreation.

"As it commands an extensive and pleasing view of a large extent of picturesque landscape, I know of no place which offers more attractions, or would be more convenient" even though several trees had recently been lost from its hedgerows.

(IP May 1882)

Dr. Norman and family.

Dr. George Blake Norman lived at Dalby House.

He was born in the old house in the field below the Park, leading on to the present Station Road. He married Miss Potter, sister to the late Samuel and Philip Potter, the noted cricketers.

The doctor made several alterations to the house, as well as enlarging it.

The surgery, which was in the yard approached from Anchor Row, was a dark, cheerless room. When I have gone sometimes on Thursday morning for medicine I have seen women sitting on forms round the surgery, waiting for Dr. Norman, who was the Public Vaccinator, to vaccinate their babies.

Dr. Norman always rode on horseback when visiting his patients.

George Blake Norman was born in March 1800, son of surgeon Samuel Blake Norman and Frances (nee Thompson).

He studied medicine in London and Paris before qualifying in 1822, from which year he practised at Ilkeston.

In October 1841 he married Sarah Potter, eldest child of coal-master and farmer Samuel and Sarah (nee East).

In 1843 he was re-appointed as Medical Officer for the Heanor District of the Basford Board of Guardians, at an annual salary of £42.

Dr. and Mrs. Norman had several children.

George Blake and Sarah Norman had ten children.

<u>Allan</u>, the eldest, was a doctor.

He married Miss Mason, ward of the Rev. James Horsburgh, who was at that time Vicar of St. Mary's.

They went to live at Monmouth, and I believe Mrs. Allan Norman died when her first baby was born.

The oldest child was physician and surgeon George Allen — perhaps named after his great-great-grandfather and Vicar of Ilkeston and Kirk Hallam.

In March 1866 he was awarded a B.A degree (Honours) at Oxford University, in December 1867 obtained the diploma of Bachelor of Medicine from the same university and shortly after began to work with his father at Dalby House.

In August 1871 he married Anne Elizabeth Mason, the daughter of farmer and land agent Charles Adnum Mason and Anne (nee Edwards). In 1849 her mother's sister Amelia Edwards had married James Horsburgh who was Vicar of St. Mary's Church (1863-1873).

Anne Elizabeth Norman died in Monmouth just over a year after her marriage and in February 1875 George Allen married his second wife, Mary Emma Moyle Smythe, daughter of army major Frederick and Ellen (nee Johnson).

In 1879 a report circulated through Ilkeston that George Allen and his wife had been *'lost at sea'* on their way to New Orleans when the steam-ship *'Memphis'* sank, with the loss of all its passengers. The ship had indeed been wrecked off the coast of Spain, near Corunna, but with no loss of life.

Blake, the second son, was also a doctor, and was assistant to his father. He married his cousin Florrie Potter, of the Park, youngest daughter of Sam Potter, the cricketer.

Like his elder brother, second son Alfred Blake Norman spent several years of education at Rossall public school at Fleetwood, Lancashire.

From Dalby House he served as a general medical practitioner and later as medical officer for the Ilkeston District of the Basford Board of Guardians, a post which he held until the end of 1874 when he left the town. (His position as medical officer was then taken by Thomas Arthur Crackle).

Alfred's marriage to Florence East Potter, second daughter of Samuel and Ann (nee Streets) and therefore his first cousin, in February 1875, was conducted at St. Mary's Church by the Rev. Alfred Potter, Rector of Keyworth and uncle to the bride and groom. After a honeymoon in Paris the couple made their home at the Market Place, Oakham, Rutland where Alfred Blake served as a general practitioner.

<u>Reginald</u> and <u>Everard</u>, the two youngest sons, went one evening to bathe in the Open Hole at Stanton; Everard was seized with cramp and was drowned.

Not present at Alfred Blake Norman's wedding in 1875 was his younger brother, by two years, Everard.

About a mile and a half from Ilkeston and formed from ironstone excavations on the estate of Colonel Newdigate, 'Open hole' at Kirk Hallam was a large pond with a depth of up to 100 feet at its centre, a popular bathing place with several private families in the area.

Everard Norman, almost 20, and his brother Reginald, 17, had often been there and were there on Wednesday afternoon, August 9th 1871, with three friends, the sons of the Rev. James Horsburgh, Vicar of Ilkeston.

It seems that Everard was swimming from the bank to reach their boat which was out on the pond, when he became disorientated and sank into the water. James Macdonald Horsburgh was alerted by the cries of his younger brother Lee who was in the boat, and from the far side of the lake he dived in and swam over to Everard, reached him but was then himself pulled under the water by his struggling friend. The two became separated and only James Macdonald reached the surface. Everard had disappeared.

The search for him continued frantically with further fruitless diving and with local people now joining in. Finally the pond had to be dragged but it wasn't until midnight that Everard's body was recovered and taken to Dalby House.

At the time of his death Everard was studying at Lincoln College, Oxford, and the Pioneer described a young man *"gifted with excellent abilities .. most commendably industrious in his studies. His character was such as to secure the admiration of all who knew him, and his pious and thoughtful habits such as afford great consolation to those who have to deplore his early death... he would in all probability have proved a useful minister in the Church of England".*

Mr W. Campbell, the toll bar keeper, made an acrostic on Everard which was printed in the local paper.

Once more, 'humble Ilkeston bard' William Campbell was moved to verse, his poem appearing in the correspondence section of the Pioneer a week after the accident.

An acrostic is a poem in which the first letter of each line spells out a word or message:

Pity young Everard met with such a fate!

Compassion bids me touch those tender strings

Which bind our hearts so close to men and things;

Those stronger chords, which form each kindred tie,

Are strangely cut, and yet we know not why;

What the design no mortal here explains,

While reason rules, or GOD his right maintains.

The Great I Am! earth trembles at His nod:

None to perfection ever found out GOD.

His ways are hid, obscure in waters deep,

Down in the sea, or on the rocky steep,

Or in the bosom of that peaceful lake

Where Norman slept, no more on earth to wake.

Calm and serene, down in the deep alone,

Himself unknowing, not to GOD unknown;

An earthly child, beneath His heavenly care

Down in that deep, the eye of GOD was there.

Then be it ours, since we must stand our lot,

To learn to trust HIM, where we trace HIM not;

And while with others we his blessings share,

Let us in friendship feel each others' care;

Mindful through life a tender heart to keep,

So shall we learn to weep with those who weep;

Deeply regret this sad bereavement here,

And freely shed the sympathetic tear,

Love and compassion both together blend

For such a son, a brother, or a friend

Mourners may wear the livery of death,

Sorrow in hope, and sigh with every breath,

Fountains of tears a thousand eyes bedim,

Yet all the world is nothing now to him.

Everard's younger brother Reginald qualified as a Member of the Royal College of Surgeons and a Licentiate of the Royal College of Physicians and subsequently married Matilda Ruth (nee Beardall?).

They spent some time in the United States and daughter Mary Ruth was born in April 1885 at Longwood, Orange County. The family later returned to live in the Skegby area. Reginald died at Sutton in Ashfield in March 1894, aged 39, and his widow then remarried to Robert Voss, town clerk solicitor in Bethnal Green, London.

<u>Edith</u> was the youngest child.

Edith was the eighth child and died at Oakham, Rutland in 1883, aged 24.

There had been other children, one girl, I think her name was Constance, died in an epidemic when about sixteen years old.

There was no Constance; this was probably <u>Sarah Jane</u>, the oldest daughter, who died from bronchitis at Dalby House in 1857, aged 13.

<u>Eleanor Gertrude</u> and <u>Cecil Mompesson</u> both died in their second year.

Youngest siblings <u>Arthur</u> and <u>Marian</u> (whooping cough) both died in infancy.

After the birth of the seventh child Dr. Norman and his family could be found taking a holiday at Bangor House, Church Walks, in Bangor, North Wales with wife Sarah's brother, the Rev. Alfred Potter.

Dr. Norman was the first chairman of the Local Board, and at one of the meetings, held at the Cricket Ground Chapel, a quarrel arose, and a free fight took place outside the chapel. It was a sad sight to see men holding prominent positions fighting like savages.

The next morning the townspeople were shocked to learn that Dr. Norman had been seized with illness. He was incapacitated and never again followed his profession.

It was always thought that the stroke was caused by the disturbance of the previous night.

Dr. Norman and his family left Ilkeston sometime later.

Adeline may be conflating two separate incidents when she recalls Dr. Norman's incapacity.

As we have seen (the Local Board's formation) the doctor was involved in the 1864 fracas at the Cricket Ground Chapel when the size of the Board was agreed. However he suffered a paralysis affecting his left side in 1869 just as he was to supervise the vote-counting at the annual election of six officers to the Local Board. This was at the time when the Board was meeting at the new Town Hall and not at the Cricket Ground Chapel.

A letter dated July 29th 1869 and written to the Local Government Office by John Wombell, as Clerk to the Board mentions that *"the gross insults the Chairman met with yesterday from the partisans of certain candidates have doubtless mainly contributed to his affliction — a severe attack of paralysis"*.

It appears that once more Dr. Norman's character had been impugned and he had been insulted about his preparations for the election; Messrs Carrier and Sudbury were among those responsible, according to the Clerk.

His incapacity led to Dr. Norman's resignation as Chairman three weeks later.

And at the end of September 1872 he left his post as Registrar of Births and Deaths to be replaced by George Barker.

With his family Dr. Norman left Ilkeston for 'The Poplars' in Manton near Oakham, Rutland in 1875.

From his appreciative patients he received a beautifully framed illuminated address.

Funds raised subsequent to his departure were sufficient to purchase an elegantly chased silver candelabrum, bearing the inscription …

"Presented to George Blake Norman, Esq., by Ilkeston friends as a token of esteem and affection. February, 1876".

Three months later the doctor was fêted by members of the Marquis of Granby Lodge of the Ilkeston and Erewash Valley United Order of Oddfellows for whom he had been the medical attendant for more than 30 years, and he was presented with 'a very handsome testimonial' or address, signed by Samuel Streets Potter, Herbert Brentnall Chadwick, Henry McDonald and John Parkinson Mee.

"The address was beautifully designed and written by R(ichard) T(homas) Mounteney, Fletcher Gate, Nottingham, on illuminated vellum, and framed in Alhambra gold, by brother I(saac) Cordon, Bath-street, Ilkeston, on whose workmanship and finish, it reflects the highest credit" (IP May 1875)

Henry George Brigham replaced Dr. Norman as medical officer for the Granby Lodge.

George Blake Norman died at his Rutland home on February 1st 1877, aged 76.

His wife Sarah died there on November 22nd 1880, aged 58.

Both were buried in the family vault in St. Mary's churchyard, near the east chancel window of the church.

"Without doubt, no man was better known in and around Ilkeston than Mr. Norman. He was a native of the town, and practised in it as a surgeon for about fifty years, during which time he won the esteem and affection of all with whom his duties brought him in contact. He has occupied many important positions in the town, and was noted for his earnestness in any good and philanthropic work. As a thorough Churchman and a staunch Conservative he has done good service to the Establishment and to his political party, and but for his death having been preceded by several years of inaction, owing to illness which had been brought on by excitement during a parochial election, his loss would have been severely felt. For many years he was Chairman of the Local Board, and indeed he occupied that office from the formation of the Board until seized by the illness above mentioned. He was also churchwarden for a long period" (NG)

The Norman Family was *"of Danish extraction, and therefore of great antiquity, as 'Burke's Landed Gentry' mentions the family at great length, and traces its ancestry to the time of Edward the Confessor".* (DM)

In May 1881 the Trustees under the will of George Blake Norman put up for sale his Ilkeston estate.

This included the *'commodious and pleasantly situated'* freehold family residence of Dalby House, including stables, large gardens and an adjoining close of pasture land of almost four acres.

Also included in the estate were ..Ÿ

….. a farm house with garden and orchard, nine cottages with gardens along Cotmanhay Road, and pasture land.

….. premises and land along the south side of Station Road some of which was occupied in 1881 by brick manufacturer Samuel Shaw. Also a dwelling house and garden on the south side of Station Road, occupied by Samuel and extending back to Chapel Street. (see Beyond North Street).

…… a Mill with attached house, gardens, stables and outbuildings, two workers' cottages, meadow land fronting up to Station Road and part of which was soon to become Mill Street.

….. also building land in this area and along both the north and south sides of Station Road.

And so to Henry George Brigham.

Dr. Brigham

Dr.Brigham was the next doctor at Dalby House.

Arrival and assimilation

Henry George Brigham, M.R.C.S., L.R.C.P., was born in Beverley, Yorkshire in 1850. Having been the resident surgeon at Victoria Hospital, London, he came to Ilkeston in September 1874 when he was taken into partnership by Dr. Norman.

In March of 1875 he married Irish-born Zanna Bayly, daughter of William and Ann, at Christ Church, Clapham.

She was a very proficient pianist and an accomplished vocalist, as evidenced at the several musical events within the district which she took part in during the couple's few years at Ilkeston.

Henry George appeared to fit immediately and seamlessly into that section of Ilkeston society previously and actively occupied by George Blake Norman.

The newly-arrived doctor gave several lectures to and prepared essays for the Ilkeston Church Mutual Improvement Society. For example in April 1876 his subject was *'Air and Water, in relation to Public Health'* given in the Boys' National school, the same lecture he had given three months before at Kirk Hallam village school-room.

The Doctor explained the nature and action of the four component gases of air (Nitrogen, Oxygen, Carbon Dioxide and the rare gases?) and proceeded to discuss the causes and evils of impure air. He spoke too of the absolute necessity of purifying water to avoid the spread of disease.

"The lecture was rendered extremely interesting by a number of experiments, in the performance of which Mr. Brigham proved himself to be a thorough master of his subject". (NG).

(On the day before and at the same place, by a show of hands, Henry George had been elected as Parish Warden over his rival Bartholomew Wilson.)

Just over a year later Henry George had prepared a *'rather lengthy'* paper on *'Nature viewed from artificial eyes'* when he brought in his own compound microscope to assist in his presentation and explain its construction to the Society. He showed slides of several vegetable and insect parts, including a spider's leg, a gnat's head, and the wing, leg and proboscis of a house fly, and tried to convey to the members of his audience the wonders which could be opened up to them through this instrument.

And at Christmas of 1877 he presented an essay on *'A few hindrances to Church work'* when he condemned the pew-letting system *'and declared himself an ardent advocate of the free and open church'.*

In the following discussion the majority of the Society concurred with his view.

(At this same meeting the Society gave formal thanks to Edwin Trueman who had just resigned as Secretary, presenting him with a fine office desk bearing a brass plate marking the occasion).

In November 1877 Dr. Brigham was elected vice-president of the newly-formed Ilkeston branch of the English Church Union.

Aneurysm and amputation

Also in November 1877 the conduct of Henry George Brigham was called into question at the inquest into the death of 15-year-old Thomas Winfield of Shortwood in Trowell. Five months earlier the lad had injured his right arm while throwing a stone and didn't know whether it was broken or out of joint. He visited a bone-setter who, on manipulating the arm, declared it 'out of joint' and promptly put it 'back in joint'. However his mother Ann (nee Stevenson) was not convinced and took Thomas to Nottingham General Hospital where a broken arm was diagnosed and a splint applied. The boy continued to visit the hospital and was eventually told he could do light work, but when the pain increased he went again to the hospital where he was examined by a surgeon. A 'next-day' appointment was made and which Thomas attended, and this was followed by another visit but each time the patient was put off by the doctors or not seen at all. Nothing was done.

When Thomas subsequently slipped and fell on his injured arm Dr. Brigham was consulted. On examining the arm, the doctor was very concerned by what he found; a circumscribed aneurysm was discovered and the lad's father, gamekeeper John Winfield, was told that an operation was required, with his permission.

The bleeding vessel inside the arm must be secured … his son's life depended on it!

What could John do?

The following day, at Thomas's home and with one assistant, Dr. Brigham operated and removed three pieces of rotten bone from the injured arm, but the prognosis was bleak. This was a very bad case and the arm would have to come off at the shoulder joint. Another day, another operation, the same patient, the same place, the same doctor — but this time, to amputate the arm.

Chloroform anaesthesia was employed and there was little loss of blood during the procedure, according to the doctor. However forty minutes later the assistant, Mr. Mollineaux, came out of the room to inform the father that Thomas 'was gone', without recovering consciousness. This assistant was qualified as such, but was not on the register of surgeons.

Dr. Brigham was sure that death was due to *'exhaustion caused by the pain Thomas was in'*, probably accelerated by the administration of chloroform, and not by the amputation.

The inquest Coroner probed the doctor. Amputation of a limb was rarely done except in hospital *"where well skilled men were found, who had a large amount of practice in such matters"*. Why had Henry George chosen to operate at the patient's home and alone? The doctor felt confident that the case was so clear, and urgent. Although the Coroner was of the opinion that this might have been an error of judgement, he didn't think that the lack of a qualified assistant surgeon had anything to do with the death. Thus the inquest jury returned a verdict and cause of death in line with the opinion expressed by the doctor.

Henry George was however very critical of the 'bone-setter' and thought he was the primary cause of the lad's death, but as Thomas had gone to him voluntarily he could not be prosecuted.

The casual approach of some of the Hospital doctors and the dismissive way in which Thomas had been treated were also criticised by the jury, and these were matters which were to be followed up.

…..and adieu

Henry George was also at this time a member of the Local Board and President of the Ilkeston and Shipley Floral and Horticultural Society; both positions he resigned in May/June 1878 when he left his practice in Ilkeston to return to London.

He was replaced at Dalby House by Dr. Samuel Armstrong, who, with his family, then lived at the house, taking out a lease for seven years.

In April 1880 Dr. Armstrong was appointed medical officer and public vaccinator for the Ilkeston district of the Basford Board of Guardians in the place of Dr. Thomas Arthur Crackle who had just died – on March 9th at Bonsall Place off Bath Street, aged 31.

At the end of 1881 Samuel and his family left Dalby House.

Into the house and into the role of public vaccinator and medical officer for the Basford Board of Guardians came James Frederick Digby Willoughby, M.R.C.S.

By 1888 lace manufacturer Charles Maltby was resident at the house and was to remain there into the next century.

Facing Dalby House across Anchor Row is the Unitarian Chapel.

This historical information kindly contributed By Dave Johnson:

Website link: **http://www.oldilkeston.co.uk/dalby-house-and-dr-norman/**

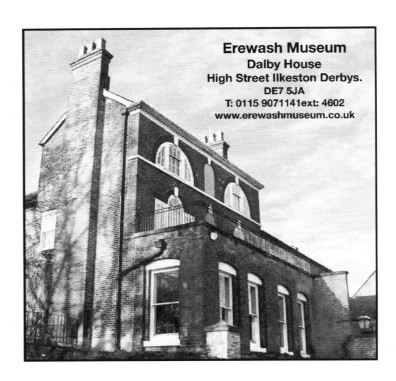

The Erewash Museum is open, right in the heart of Ilkeston and has an excellent website giving full details of opening and closing times: **www.erewashmuseum.co.uk**

It is a free-social history Museum, founded in the 1980's and is situated in Dalby House, a much extended Georgian dwelling that has been a family home and a school in years gone by. Even though it is now a museum the house has retained many of it's original features, and having been the recipient of a National Lottery Grant and being supported by Erewash Borough Council, it's future would seem more secure. However the management are not complacent, and Erewash museum became **'Derbyshire Museum of the year in 2011, 2012 and 2016', winners of the 'Excellence Award' at the East Midlands Heritage Awards and winners of The Sandford Award for Heritage Education.**

Having recently made another joint visit, along with Brian Fretwell, I believe Erewash Museum to shine as a bright jewel in the Borough's crown. There is a Victorian kitchen, a 1950'a sweetshop, a mining room, war gallery and Stanton gallery, not to mention the masses of incidental, eye-opening, special displays, posters and exhibits. It is a veritable wonderland of social history and should be a 'must visit' for tourists and locals' alike.

Harry Riley

Museum Shop

Dalby House Museum Range

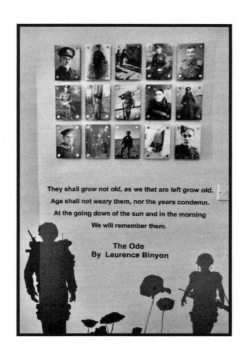

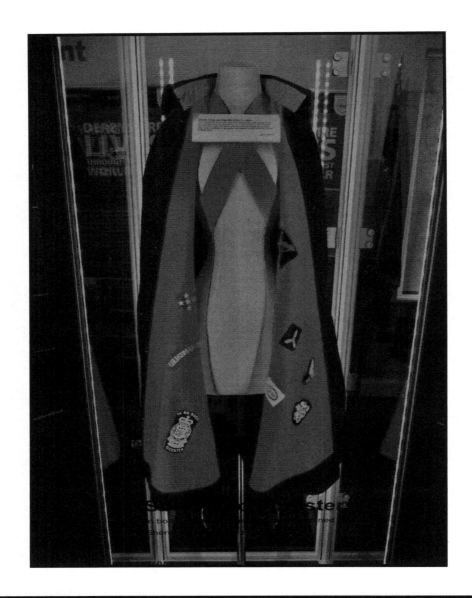

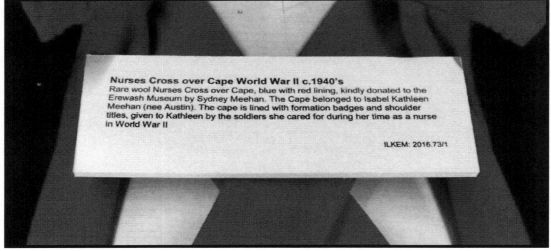

Nurses Cross over Cape World War II c.1940's
Rare wool Nurses Cross over Cape, blue with red lining, kindly donated to the Erewash Museum by Sydney Meehan. The Cape belonged to Isabel Kathleen Meehan (nee Austin). The cape is lined with formation badges and shoulder titles, given to Kathleen by the soldiers she cared for during her time as a nurse in World War II

ILKEM: 2016.73/1

Erewash Museum Poster

Harry Riley Review
An Event in The D. H. Lawrence Festival of Culture
'THE COUNTRY OF MY HEART.'
VENUE: ST. MARY'S CHURCH GREASLEY
Sun. 10th Sept. 2017

Given by Alan Wilson (organ and piano) together with readings narrated by Well-known Screen Actor: Wayne Foskett, supported by David Amos, Fred Skillington, Jackie Greaves, and Ann Whyte; the whole programme introduced by Eastwood D.H. Lawrence Society Chairman: Malcolm Gray

If, like me, (a lapsed churchgoer) you believed a church organ was simply a powerful means of providing 'Sombre' and 'high-falutin' wedding and funeral music/marches, then this concert would have been a truly remarkable eye-opener.

This was a concert of 3 sections, with a mid-way interval; and we were treated to a lively programme of music and readings dedicated to several locally famous and inspiring luminaries: David Herbert Lawrence, (author) George Gordon Byron, (poet) Eric Coates, (composer) and William Hopkin (poet.)

Any doubtful feelings I might have had, of sitting in a drafty church, on back-breakingly-upright, hard-pews for 3 hours, were quickly dispelled, as this enchanting sequence of music, poems and readings began.

Not only did Alan Wilson shatter all my own taboos about church organ music, but he produced classical and (own composition) arrangements, making this ancient Organ sing and dance, soaring to great heights, even replicating Birds twittering: 'The Song of the Birds,' as a member of this packed audience was later heard to say.

Here was a magical, modern-day-maestro at work, paying tribute to our late great, champions.

In-between, we had superb readings of Prose and Poetry from Wayne Foskett, Jackie Greaves, Ann Whyte, David Amos and Fred Skillington.

All contributors, led by Alan Wilson, were rapturously applauded for a fine afternoon of original entertainment.
Alan was thanked By Malcolm Gray, and asked to come back, as he received a token of appreciation from Ruth Hall of the D.H. Lawrence Society.

'THE COUNTRY OF MY HEART'

An organ concert, in association with the D.H Lawrence Society and generously supported by Liberty Leisure as part of the D H Lawrence Festival of Culture, celebrating music connected with the three 'greats': Lawrence, Byron and Coates

At
St. Mary's Church, Greasley (NG16 2AB)
On
Sunday 10th September 2017 at 3 p.m.

Given by Alan Wilson

Alan Wilson, Organist of St. Mary-le-Bow, London (the famous 'Bow Bells' church) and former Director of Music at Queen Mary University of London, returns to his roots, recalling a rich tapestry of local gems, played on a fine historic organ in this atmospheric country church.

Tickets £5, including refreshments, available at the door. Please let us know if you wish to attend by emailing Brenda on: brenda.sumner@gmail.com
Or by phoning Ruth on 07875121936

(The church will be open to the public, as part of the Festival, on:
Saturday 9th September – 10-12 noon
Sunday 10th September – 12-2 p.m.)

All welcome

Alan Wilson (Bio)

Alan Wilson, born 1947 in Giltbrook, just outside Eastwood, came from a chiefly mining family, through several generations, as well as a musical one, fostered by his grandfather, Billie Burrows and uncle John Wilson, the latter being organist at St. Mary's Langley and supporting organist at Heanor Parish Church. Alan spent a very happy childhood in Eastwood, attending Beauvale School and Eastwood Hall Park and Eastwood Baptist Church (Where he was organist), before going to the Royal College of Music on a scholarship. He studied Piano, organ, harpsichord and composition, then winning another scholarship to study organ and harpsichord in Amsterdam with Gustav Leonhardt, a leading authority on Early Keyboard Music.

Alan has spent a lifetime in the field of music. As well as being Director of Music at Queen Mary University of London (1976-2013), Director of Music/Organist at London University Church of Christ the King (1973-86), and at St. Mary-Le-Bow, London (from 1986), he also was a member of the highly acclaimed Early Music group 'The Consort of Musicke' for many years. He is well known internationally as a published composer of predominately church choral and organ music, as well as still being active as a recitalist. He is an Honary Associate of the Royal School of Church Music and is one of the Musical Directors of the BBC Radio Daily Service.

Sandiacre Lock Cottages

By Glyn Stenson

The cottages were built around 1779 at Sandiacre Lock on the Erewash Canal.

Although each of the 13 locks along the twelve and three-quarter miles length of the canal had a lock cottage attached, Sandiacre lock cottages are the only ones that remain today. The Erewash Canal extends from the Langley Mill, Great Northern Basin to the River Trent at Sawley. The cottages at Sandiacre housed the families of the canal maintenance and also the lock and Toll House keepers. When the canal first opened, industry along the Erewash Canal was extremely busy and sometimes hectic. The movement of commerce along the canal included coal, stone and iron products as examples. Links with a network of other canals and the River Trent meant goods could be easily distributed around the country.

Sandiacre Lock was particularly important as it linked with the Derby Canal and you can still see where the two canals once joined. The Derby Canal was abandoned and subsequently filled in during the early 1970s, however, there are plans for renovation and re-opening.

The Sandiacre Lock Cottages has a Toll House which is still preserved today. During its commercial heyday, owners of barges moving freight along the canal paid a fee for the privilege of using the canal. The charge depended on the weight of the goods being transported !

In the late 1960s the cottages were under threat of demolition as they were deemed uninhabitable and the Erewash Canal was also under the threat of closure. The Erewash Canal Preservation and Development Association (ECP&DA) was formed in 1968 and the group restored large sections of the canal and the cottages. The ECP&DA remains today and continues to thrive with over 200 members. The association celebrated its 50th birthday in January 2018 ! We look forward to a prosperous future and continuing the good work to enable boaters to navigate the canal, walkers and cyclists to enjoy the towpaths.

Today the cottages, which are two cottages merged into one, remain relatively unspoilt and people can visit free of charge to glimpse the canal's historic heritage (see ECP&DA website for days, times and contact). Community and education groups are also welcome to access the cottages at times to suit. Future cottages opening will include themed events for all the family for example: Victorian wash days, ragging (rug making), bobbin lace, ships in bottles, decorative rope work and our special Christmas openings with decorated cottages using traditional, natural foliage.

R. I. P. Keith Longdon. Born 9th August 1944 –died 3rd January 2018

Keith was well-known and liked for his community work around Eastwood both by the elderly and the youth of the town. He worked tirelessly for Eastwood Parish (being a former Mayor of Eastwood and Nottinghamshire Councillor.) His funeral was extremely well attended with a fine eulogy given by close friend and Broxtowe Councillor Mrs. Josie Masters.

Keith Longdon: David Townes: Sarah Taylor

Tribute to Jackie Trent

On 21st March 2015 Jackie Trent, Internationally renowned singer and songwriter and the great, late 'Patron' of Eastwood Booktown Development Group, died in Menorca aged 74. Only a few months earlier I 'David Page' had met up again with Jackie and Colin, her Nottingham-born husband in the grounds of Kingsmill Hospital, to escort them to the Millside Radio Studio where Jackie was to do a special recording with presenter Charlie Brown, for the hospital ward patients.

Jackie's husband-Colin takes up the story: 'This was 'business as usual' for Jackie; for many years she was an Ambassador for Variety International – The Childrens' Charity, raising millions of precious dollars for disabled and disadvantaged children around the world; always having loads of fun, of course! 'That was Jackie Trent's trademark, and is her legacy:

Bringing fun, Happiness and Entertainment to her millions of adoring fans'

Colin continues... 'Jackie Trent hailed from Staffordshire, and after moving to London at an early age enjoyed a glittering career in show business. But she sought adventure, so Jackie packed her bags and signed up to entertain the troops under fire: in occupied Europe, The Middle East, the Trucial States, Turkey and Africa...

Still a 'minor,' her parents even had to give their permission for their 16-year old daughter to go abroad. Twice, in Cyprus, she narrowly escaped certain death from being blown up by EOKA landmines; others died at the time...

'But destiny drew Jackie back onto the conventional stage in life: her incredible voice and dazzling beauty – her charisma – won her millions of fans.

Tony Hatch, the songwriter, was attracted too: they married in 1967; moved over to Southern Ireland, then Australia, where they became known as Mr. and Mrs. Australia. Jackie had top hits with 'My Love,' 'Colour My World,' 'Don't Sleep In The Subway' and her No.1 in the charts: 'Where Are You Now My Love.'

Over a period of time they had written songs for Shirley Bassey, Frank Sinatra, Dean Martin, Sammy Davis Junior, Petula Clark, amongst other top musical performers, and for television they created the 'Neighbours' theme tune. Eventually, several decades later, after divorcing Tony Hatch, Jackie moved to Spain, meeting and marrying Colin Gregory.

'Jackie carried on with her charity work for Servicemen and Women and continued travelling to Australia for annual 'Forces Remembrance services such as Anzac Day parades. It was during her recording work for Forces 'Heroes' that she contacted me to include my (Harry Riley) 'Remembrance poem' for Armistice Day and I was only too pleased to agree. Not long afterwards Jackie and Colin accepted my invitation to spend a weekend with our Eastwood Book-Town Community Group at Eastwood, and to visit Durban House; D. H. Lawrence and Mining Heritage Centre, to meet children from Eastwood Comprehensive School.

Both Jackie and Colin's relatives had been miners and the subject was close to their hearts.

Jackie Trent

The Official Website of the Singer & Songwriter

Home   2014 News   Gigs   Discography   Guestbook   Fans   Shop   Contact

Armistice & Remembrance

Remembrance Day 2014

Not so very long ago – 28 July 1914 – the guns of war erupted over Europe, inexorably bringing death and destruction to the World. Meantime, Tsar 'Nicky' and Kaiser 'Willy' wrote to each other - 8 telegrams over 4 short days - as the Generals mobilised their forces...

And who actually suffered?
He did, for one:
Remember me
Duty called and I went to war
Though I'd never fired a gun before
I paid the price for your new day
As all my dreams were blown away

Remember me
We all stood true as whistles blew
And faced the shell and stench of Hell
Now battle's done, there is no sound
Our bones decay beneath the ground
We cannot see, or smell, or hear
There is no death, or hope or fear

Remember me
Once we, like you, would laugh and talk
And run and walk and do the things that you all do
But now we lie in rows so neat
Beneath the soil, beneath your feet

Remember me
In mud and gore and the blood of war
We fought and fell and move no more
Remember me, I am not dead
I'm just a voice within your head...
Remember Me
(The voice of the dead)
Harry Riley

276

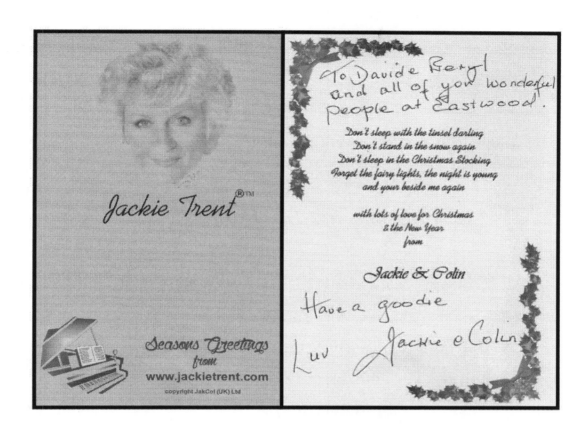

Jackie Trent ®™

Seasons Greetings
from
www.jackietrent.com
copyright JakCol (UK) Ltd

To David e Beryl
and all of you wonderful
people at Eastwood.

Don't sleep with the tinsel darling
Don't stand in the snow again
Don't sleep in the Christmas Stocking
Forget the fairy lights, the night is young
and your beside me again

with lots of love for Christmas
& the New Year
from

Jackie & Colin

Have a goodie
Luv Jackie e Colin

RIP Jackie... David Page

Lloyd Binch, Cycling Champion
of Kimberley Notts.
By his daughter: Debbie Binch

At the tender age of 3, Lloyd's dad put him on a 3 wheeled bike in the backyard and told him to pedal fast. Lloyd pedalled and hit the garden wall at full pelt, ending up in a heap in the flower bed. But this did not put him off cycling. He swopped the 3-wheeler for a 2-wheeler and found that he could go fast! As a teenager, he joined Notts Castle Bicycle Club and was soon taking part in and winning races, starting on grass tracks. His first experience of hard-track racing was on the old Derby Municipal cement track where the sport was booming at that time and mid-week league meetings with Reg Harris, Sid Patterson and Alan Bannister among the guest riders were pulling in good crowds, and Lloyd and other local riders like Eric Thompson, Wally Box, Jim Turner and Ron Meadwell were putting an edge on their speed. He jumped from obscurity to world-championship racing in little more than a year.

During the following decade Lloyd won the British 1000 metre sprint title seven times in succession, a feat unequalled in the annals of British cycling. He won the Grand Prix sprint events of most European capitals from Paris to Prague and Berlin to Copenhagen. An example of his determination was when with arms bandaged, and his back in plaster, he took on and beat by inches the French champion Andre Gruchet who at one stage was 10 lengths ahead. He said that losing never entered his head when he entered the track. Despite this single-mindedness, in later life he rarely spoke about these achievements. In addition to shattering records all over Europe, his independent attitude to those in authority earned him the sports page title of "Rebel of the Handlebars".

Although he raced in the Commonwealth and Olympic games, the thing he constantly recalled with most pleasure was the Sunday Club runs to Derbyshire. Two bob covered the day, and part of the fun was sprinting for the road signs. The local track Harvey Haddon Stadium was where Lloyd spent a lot of time, but later his dad bought a car to enable Lloyd to get down to the Herne Hill track in London, and to the Fallowfield track in Manchester. The family home always seemed full of young cyclists from all over the world, all welcomed by Lloyd's parents Leslie and Margaret.

While racing, Lloyd worked for Raleigh testing bikes to their limits, and on retiring from the track, Lloyd was offered a job at the new Moulton Bicycle Company promoting this new small-wheeled bike. In a Mini, with three bikes mounted on top, Lloyd travelled the country from Lands End to John O' Groats. After retiring from cycling, Lloyd played golf and then bowls, and in later life, he loved listening to his music, dog walking, and enjoying the garden, even when his health started to fail.

Lloyd was born on 28th August 1931 in Kimberley and died on 15th December 2016 in Kimberley.

Lloyd's victory lap after winning the Forst Grand Prix in 1959

Lloyd's 'Fallowfield' Presentation

Lloyd's victory at Harvey Haddon Stadium

ST. HELEN'S CHURCH TROWELL HISTORY

Rev. Dr. Andy Lord

It was AD 801 when Trowell was a tiny Saxon settlement in the kingdom of Mercia that permission was given for a church, made from wood and wattle, to be built at the request of the people. In 1080 the church was re-constructed from local sandstone on the same site, with the Doomsday Book saying: "Here is a priest and half a church and six acres of meadow." Traces of the ancient building are still clearly visible, especially in the large archway in the south wall of the present chancel. For some unknown reason the church was largely rebuilt a 100 years later. What is now the chancel would have been the whole church at that time.

Since the 12th century there have been many changes and additions in response to the requirements and traditions of succeeding generations. The nave, aisles and eventually the clerestory were added during the following 300 years. An embattled tower, completed in 1480, contains six bells, originally cast in 1792 and re-cast by Taylors of Loughborough in 1931.

Originally there would have been little or no seating in the nave. Box pews, installed in the 1770s, were removed in 1836 and replaced with chairs. It was only when the church underwent a major re-fit in 1891 to raise the chancel floor, that pews and other furnishings were re-instated.

From early times until the end of the 19th century, the church was heated by coal stoves and oil lamps provided the lighting. In the Middle Ages, the church building would have been the only community building in the village and in common with most other village churches it would have hosted many events, meetings and festivals other than Sunday worship. Nave seating, if any, at that time would have been moveable benches. The chancel is where the worship would have taken place, with the congregation mostly standing and looking on from the nave. It was only in Victorian times that churches became reserved for worship alone.

The pulpit dates back to the 1891 restoration and replaced "a quaint old wooden pulpit bearing the date 1667". The font is a large 14th century octagonal font with a quatrefoil in each panel, an embattled edge and also quatrefoils around the base. In 1927 the old Nottingham Exchange clock was placed in the tower at the expense of Mr. S. P. Derbyshire as a memorial to his grandparents who had lived in the house immediately to the east of the church (The old Rectory House of the First Mediety). The clock was hand-wound until the early 1970's when an electric motor was fitted. The organ was presented by the late Mr William Smith (founder of the local firm of corn millers) in 1900. The organ was originally worked by hand, a person behind the organ in the ringing chamber operated a lever to pump the bellows.

The church contains only one ancient monument and that is to the memory of William Hacker who was buried under the altar on 22nd December 1668. The Latin inscription describes him as "a most obedient son of the Church of England. He was the light and pillar of Trowell whilst he lived." His nephew was the Colonel Francis Hacker who was convicted of high treason and hanged as a traitor at Tyburn. Other members of the Hacker family are buried in the south aisle of the nave. The memorial window at the east end of the north aisle is in memory of the men of Trowell who died in the 1939–45 war and the stained glass window on the east side of the south aisle is in memory of the son of a Rector of Trowell, the Revd E. J. R. Nichols, who was killed in the Great War 1914–1918.

In 2012 there was a desire to install a modern, energy efficient heating system which would keep the church warm, even in the coldest winter weather. An enthusiastic sub committee soon realised that renewal of the heating system offered opportunities to make the church more adaptable to modern needs. This became known as the Renewal Project. The existing heating system, installed about 1900, was built round the church furnishings in several areas and was originally powered by a coal-fired boiler. A gas boiler was added 50 years ago but never achieved severe weather performance, even after being switched on for five or six hours before a service started. It was known that the old pipes, radiators and header tank would soon start to give serious trouble. Clear evidence of advanced corrosion could at any time lead to serious water damage in the building.

Small choir stalls, originally built for choir boys, severely limited the capacity and usefulness of the chancel area, which, in recent years, had become little used. A review revealed that at some time during the 1950s much of the nave furniture had been subject to an attack of woodworm. Considerable wood rot and beetle infestation had also made some pews unsafe until repairs were carried out about six years ago. The nave floor was of stone slabs with a herring-bone ceramic block pattern in the pew areas. Some blocks had become broken and loose or were missing, forming a trip hazard. Originally the chancel floor was at the same level as the nave floor but in 1890 it was raised up two steps as was traditional at that time. However, this made it more difficult for the less able to get to the altar rail. Also the large stained glass east window was partially obscured by the reredos screen.

Hence the plans went forward to provide a new heating system, level the floor throughout, replace the pews with comfortable chairs and install a new audio-visual system. This required meetings with Diocesan and national bodies responsible for church buildings. The desire has been to keep the ancient nature of the church building whilst enabling it to better serve the community of today. St Helen's has hosted regular drop-ins, coffee mornings, children's events and arts & flower festivals. The renewal scheme enables these to be developed and for the church to host other events for the community. The vision of St Helen's over the last decade has been to "walk with Jesus by the Spirit in community." There is a recognition of the way in which Jesus draws community together and enables service through the giving of the Holy Spirit of love. Here a deepening Christian faith requires a wider engagement with the concerns and issues of those beyond the church. It is Jesus who draws together the past, present and future together in hope and action. This ancient church is now moving ahead to become a warm and welcoming beacon for future generations.

A special service, led by the Bishop of Southwell and Nottingham, the Rt. Rev. Tony Porter, was held on January 14th 2018 to celebrate the completion of the Renewal Project. As well as benefiting from efficient economical heating, the new insulated floor is at one level right through to the communion rail giving full disabled access. A new glazed oak outer door at the porch replaces the old iron gate. A new audio / music system is installed complete with an induction loop facility for hearing aid users and the video / data projection system is unique in the village for community use. The new altar table and lectern designs are the result of ideas developed by the project committee. Two reader's desks and the pulpit desk have been made from reclaimed oak.

Further work is anticipated that will tackle issues involving power and lighting, the vestry / crèche, some internal stonework, cleaning of the nave walls and the restoration of historical and heritage features. The whole scheme will cost about £180,000, of which a significant portion is being raised by the congregation in direct giving and fund raising efforts, with the rest coming from grants. The church has been grateful to everyone who has pulled together and given generously to make this happen.

The Rector through this renewal project has been the Revd Dr Andy Lord who has been at St Helen's since 1996. Andy drifted from Christian faith as a teenager as he saw Christian faith being about something in a special building on Sundays but little connected with the wider life of the community and world. At University he encountered Christians whose faith motivated their involvement in world issues, travelling to help the poorest in the world. Perhaps Christian faith had more to it than he imagined! This led Andy to study afresh the Bible and debate with others, finally seeking to follow Jesus afresh himself. For many years Andy worked in computers but gradually felt God nudging him to other things. Thus five years were spent working for a Christian mission organisation that sought to bring good into a world of complex difficulties. Then followed training in Cambridge for ordination and a curacy in four rural churches in Peterborough Diocese. Andy has maintained the desire to connect Christian faith with ordinary life in community, as well as to deepen his faith through prayer and study. He has completed an MA and PhD in theology and has written three books exploring the nature of the church and its mission and renewal. As well as being Rector in Trowell he is also Rector in Cossall and Awsworth and has overseen the renewal of Cossall Community Hall and a new heating project in Awsworth. He says, "It has been a real joy and challenge to serve the churches and communities in Trowell, Cossall and Awsworth these last 11 years. To be involved in the celebrations and losses of many peoples lives has been a real privilege. Leading people to the Father of mercies and Jesus of all compassion in the love of the Holy Spirit is a precious calling. For me, buildings work has been a real learning experience! But together much has been achieved."

St Helen's Trowell is a church with a rich heritage that is looking forwards to serving the community in the many years to come.

St. Helen's Trowell before the 2017 Reordering

St. Helen's Trowell after the 2017 Reordering

Trowell C of E Primary School Choir Singing at St. Helen's for a Special Open Day

Andy Lord with Bishop Tony at the Dedication Service for St. Helen's after the Renewal Project

The Early Church at Trowell

Trowell Church is a Grade 2 star listed building which has been on the site for many hundreds of years, in fact the first recorded reference to it may be found in the annals of York Minster, where it states that "An application was made by the Lord of the Manor in Trowell, for a Church to be established, at the request of the people." Trowell was then probably a Saxon settlement.

Permission was granted in 801, which means that a Church may have been on this site for nearly 1200 years. Traces of the Saxon church are reputed to have been found under the present chancel. The next reference to the church is in the Domesday Book which quotes "Here is a priest and half a church and six acres of meadow". This was valued in the Confessor's time (1046) at 100 shillings; but in the Conqueror's time when the Domesday Book was written (1080) at 20 shillings.

> **NOTE:** *The reference to "a priest and half a church" means that it was shared with another parish; in the case of Trowell, this was Cossall and the Rectors of Trowell received half the tythes of Cossall, this continued until they were commuted in 1787.*

Chancel

The present chancel dates back to 1180, which is a very early example of Early English architecture, the fabric consisting of untrimmed masonry in thin courses. By this date Trowell was a well developed parish with a population of fifty.

The lancet windows, filled-in priest's door, and a filled in archway which was to an earlier side chapel can be seen in these pictures.

The piscina, credence, and sedilia also date from this earlier period. A piscina is a small niche which was used to hold a bowl of water where the priest washed his hands during a service of communion (also called mass). The credence shelf is another small niche with a shelf on which were placed the bread and wine used during the communion. The sedilia are a group of three seats on the south wall of the sanctury in which the clergy would sit during high mass. The church was originally Roman Catholic like all of the other churches in England but became Protestant when Henry VIII separated from the Pope and became head of the Church of England. The windows in the south wall are of Perpendicular insertion.

Until 1890 the east window contained painted glass, which was replaced with a stained glass window by Kemp. This window is dedicated in memory of the Revd Robert John Hodgkinson 1888-90. A reredos was erected three feet from the east wall to allow the priest to have room to robe up. A new altar table, altar rail, new oak choir seats and chancel screen were introduced and the chancel floor raised at the 1890 restoration. In the Robert Thoroton Histories, it is stated that the chancel had contained monuments which had been mutilated during the Puritan period, but by early in the 19th century they had been removed.

When William Stretton of Lenton visited St. Helen's in 1818, he describes the east window - of five lights in two storeys which had been beautifully ornamented with painted glass of a superior kind, fragments of which still remain, a label to a mutilated figure is inscribed 'EDW T REX'. He describes the chancel floor as being bad, and the Priest's door was still in place.

Nave

The nave and side aisles were added in the 14th century, these were built in Trowell sandstone; the arcade of three arches each side of the nave are also of this date. The walls were raised in the 15th century and three two-light clerestory windows inserted each side. The square headed windows on the outer walls of the aisles are of interest since they are only to be found in parts of Nottinghamshire and Derbyshire.

The pulpit only dates back to the 1891 restoration and replaced "a quaint old wooden pulpit bearing the date 1667".

The memorial window at the east end of the north aisle is in memory of the men of Trowell who died in the 1939–45 war and the stained glass window on the east side of the south aisle is in memory of the son of a Rector of Trowell, the Revd E. J. R. Nichols, who was killed in the Great War 1914–1918.

Font

The font is a large 14th century octagonal font with a quatrefoil in each panel, an embattled edge and also quatrefoils around the base.

Porch

The 14th century porch retains the stone vault supported by four arch ribs on either side, but restoration work during the last 150 years has taken away most of its ancient characteristics.

Tower & Bells

The tower, completed in 1480, is also built entirely of Trowell sandstone, and is a two-staged embattled tower.

From 1480 to 1792 there were only three bells in the tower, but in 1792 six bells were cast by Taylors of Loughborough and fitted. In 1931 the bells were re-cast, again by Taylors. The bells range in size from 2'1" to 3'0" (63 - 91.5cm) in diameter and 3.64 to 9.25cwts (185 - 470kg). Each bell carries an inscription which was reproduced when the bells were re-cast.

The top of the tower, which is reached by a steep spiral staircase, gives fantastic views of the area on a fine day.

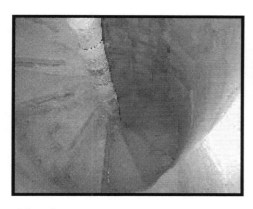

Clock

In 1927 the old Nottingham Exchange clock was placed in the tower at the expense of Mr. S. P. Derbyshire as a memorial to his grandparents who had lived in the house immediately to the east of the church. (The old Rectory House of the First Mediety). The clock was hand-wound until the early 1970's when an electric motor was fitted.

Organ

The organ was presented by the late Mr William Smith (founder of the local firm of corn millers) in 1900. The organ was originally worked by hand, a person behind the organ in the ringing chamber operated a lever to pump the bellows.

Restoration

From time to time the church has been extensively restored. In 1835 at the expense of Lord Middleton, all the old painted glass which contained fragments of the Brinsley and Strelley coat of arms was taken out; all tracery and mullions were cut out of the nave and aisle windows, and the walls were thickly plastered. This covered up The Commandments, Lord's Prayer and Creed, painted in 1777 by Samuel Pinkney, then Churchwarden. The flat oak roof was lathed and plastered.

Further restoration work in 1890, involved new roofs for both chancel and nave, the plaster was removed from the nave, the windows restored and oak pews were fitted in the nave. A choir vestry was formed in the lower part of the tower beneath  a ringing chamber which was raised some nine feet above the vestry floor.

Restoration re-commenced in 1956, this work consisted of replacing some of the outside face of the nave and the tower walls with Derbyshire gritstone. This work will need to continue until all the Trowell sandstone has been covered.

Monuments
The church contains only one ancient monument and that is to the memory of William Hacker who was buried under the altar on 22nd December 1668. The Latin inscription describes him as "a most obedient son of the Church of England. He was the light and pillar of Trowell whilst he lived." His nephew was the Colonel Francis Hacker who was convicted of high treason and hanged as a traitor at Tyburn. Other members of the Hacker family are buried in the south aisle of the nave.

Various other plaques and brasses recording burials in the church are located on the walls and floor. One commemorating the Reverend Tristram Exley who died in 1792 and who is buried in the chancel, is hidden behind the altar.

Trowell Benefice
Records show that the patronage was originally held by William Peverel from the time of the Conquest until 1241, when the Convent of Sempringham became patron. The patronage was taken over by the Crown in 1550, following the dissolution of the monasteries at the time of Henry VIII. The Crown remained patron until 1588, when the Willoughby family purchased the patronage.

In 1259 the Brinsley family applied for a dispensation to hold an additional "Benefice with cure of souls". From then on Trowell Church came under two Patrons and two Rectors. The two halves were called the First Mediety and the Second Mediety. The Crown remained patron of the First Mediety and the Brinsley family were patrons of the Second Mediety. (In some records the name Brinsley is spelt Brunnesley).

The Brinsley family held the patronage of the Second Mediety until it was purchased by the Hacker family in 1602. The First Mediety remained with the Willoughby family until 1724 when Lord Middleton became Patron. Lord Middleton then became Patron of the whole church in 1787, when the two halves were re-united

The Parish Registers do not begin until 1570 but it is obvious that some leaves must be missing as the statement on the flyleaf quotes 1558. The Register is of parchment and on the flyleaf is written:

"In this booke, is contayned the names of those that have been maride, babtissed and buried from the firste year of the reigne of the Queenes moste excellent Majestie Elizabethe, by the grace of God of England and France. The Queene, defender of the faythe, etc. untyll this present, beinge the fortythe of her graces Raigne and the year of our lord god 1598"

Nicholas Hallam, Thomas Slacke Rectors

The date 1598 would be that in which the present register was transcribed from the original paper book.

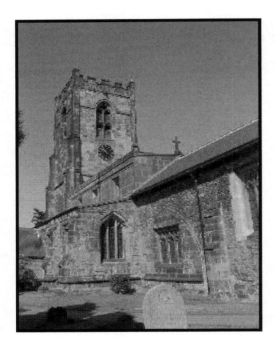

St. Helen's Today	
This picture shows evidence of changes through time	
1180	Chancel
	Archway to side chapel
C14	Nave
C15	Nave walls raised
1480	Tower
1914/18	Memorial window
1927	Clock
1956	Stonework restoration
1999	Chancel re-roofed in Welsh slate
Alan J Cook - December 1999 Photographs by Joan & Don Whysall	

Alan John Wilson, was born on 26th May 1947 on Portland Road, Giltbrook, though the family soon moved to a larger house on Nottingham Road towards Hill Top. He comes from a mining family going back many generations. This applies to both mother's side and father's, though his father was a hosiery operator in the nearby (now defunct) flourishing factory Aristoc. There was however strong music in the family; especially mother's father and father's elder brother, John. Billy Burrows, Alan's grandpa, was a chief winder at Moorgreen Colliery and a very enthusiastic amateur musician, exercising immense influence on Alan's childhood. The old house, also on Nottingham road, was full of music, and in the 'front room' (the 'posh room') was a piano and a harmonium. Even at the age of four the infant Alan would be heard improvising on the piano and grandpa would delight the family most Sunday evenings with hymn singing around the harmonium. Billy Burrows was also a keen violist, playing in the local 'Lyric' orchestra. Uncle John was the other key genetic and influential music contributor to the young Alan. John was a fine devoted church musician, most of his life being organist and choirmaster at St Mary's Langley (on Holbrook street, building now sadly demolished) and was assistant organist at Heanor Parish Church of St. Lawrence. He was also a very skilled carpenter – later on, along with Alan's father, he built one of Alan's keyboard instruments (a spinet). Uncle John's passion for organ music was immense, and this was certainly carried through into Alan's DNA. Alan recalls one time when he was a student at the Royal College of Music, recording an improvisation on a big three manual organ in London, and on playing this to his uncle on his Grundig TK 20 tape recorder, discovered uncle John moved to tears saying 'I was right there with you on every note!' Alan frequently even now, along with John's daughter Sylvia, reminisces about the immense gratitude and admiration he had for his charismatic uncle.

Alan began his education at the famous and historic Beauvale Primary school.

From there he went to Mansfield Technical Grammar School (later renamed Sherwood Hall Boys School) and in the sixth form was transferred to Eastwood Hall Park School. He also won an award to attend the newly formed Nottinghamshire Music School, and among several studies was privileged to have piano tuition with the much revered Holly Slaney. Alan remembers her as a strict but very kind teacher. She suffered no nonsense, expecting high standards and diligence, but was immensely generous in giving extra tuition when required. Many of her pupils, including Alan, would be chief prize winners in all sorts of competitions. The Saturday music school, created and led by Dr. Arthur Veal, gave a firm foundation for what was to become Alan's career. His time at Mansfield school was a happy (and hard working) one, but the distance of travel and the required commitments to after school rehearsals, along with early mornings and late evening's homework, proved too much for the young boy and that is why a transfer to the sixth form at local Eastwood was necessary. Alan remembers with affection there the music teacher David Wigley.

Along with his musical education, Alan's involvement in the family church, Eastwood Baptist, played another formative part. Church attendance was obligatory in the family, marking three times on a Sunday. Every year would be held a church's mega festival called the 'Sunday School Anniversary'. To a packed church, music was led by choirmaster Fred Smith, another influential person to Alan. After a normal Sunday evening's service, Alan would frequently be invited to Fred's home to hear his latest vinyl record purchase of some big orchestral symphonic work played on his prized hi-fi set. The other person Alan owes immense gratitude to was the Minister during that time, the Reverend John Leigh, who firmly moulded Alan in a spiritual direction. John Leigh survived well into his nineties and Alan was so touched to be asked to play at his Thanksgiving Service of Commemoration comparatively recently.

The next stage of Alan's life took him down south to London, and he was never to return to Eastwood as a resident, though as will be explained later, he does regard Eastwood as his second home with many new projects forthcoming.

Thanks again to Holly Slaney's exceptional teaching, Alan won a piano scholarship to the Royal College of Music, along with a 'silver medal' for outstanding achievement in Associated Board Exam Finals. Here he entered a musical paradise. His chief study was piano with Phyllis Sellick, who along with her husband Cyril Smith, was a leading pianist and teacher at the College. For his second study Alan chose harpsichord.

Through the charismatic influence of Dr. Thornton Lofthouse (known affectionately as 'Lofty') this was soon to take precedence in shaping Alan's future. Alan also became an organ pupil of Nicholas Danby, who was well known in the field of organ scholarship and research. 'Early Music', so called, was still in its infancy in the 1960's, but thanks to both Lofthouse and Danby, this paved the way for the next stage of Alan's education: that was to win a further scholarship to study organ and harpsichord with the internationally acclaimed Gustav Leonhardt at the Amsterdam Conservatorium. Leonhardt, a top musicologist, was the greatest exponent of early keyboard and ensemble music at that time, and to be able to study with him was indeed a high honour. Alan was also indebted to his music theory professor, John Lambert, for encouraging him to take up formal composition lessons (he had already been writing music since childhood) and as well as receiving fine teaching from Lambert, it led to special master classes with the infamous French teacher Nadia Boulanger.

Life in Amsterdam in the late sixties was a cultural wonder. Everyone seemed to love music. Alan even recalls the milkman whistling Bach and the wine bars would be resounding to the dancing baroque music of Telemann and Vivaldi! The art galleries, churches, canals, organs, and of course the charisma of Leonhardt all moulded Alan into a firm love of high culture. Here he also experienced his first major post as choir master, as he led the choir in the English speaking Anglican Church in Amsterdam.

But this was soon to change. On returning to London he now had to cease being a student and to look for employment. He was slowly able to pick up the odd gig of concert playing but he really needed a stable teaching commitment. This signaled an unusual turn in Alan's development. He was initially engaged as piano tutor at the challenging 'Trinity House Girls School' in the then very rough area of the Elephant and Castle, London. He was told that 'no one survived here more than a few months' and the Head of Music suddenly left. Alan was asked at short notice to take over the running of the music here. It was indeed a challenge – discipline was unstable, and the pupils had no interest in the music Alan had been accustomed to.

But then something quite remarkable happened. Alongside his classical training, Alan had always had an interest in pop music, and thanks to interesting conversations with some of the sixth formers, he decided to find out more about this genre. He would frequently listen to the top twenty every Sunday evening, work out arrangements, and then get the pupils to sing these in class alongside a bit of theory popped in here and there. He formed a choir and before long was turning his compositional skills to the writing of pop/rock cantatas. The success of this choir, not only provided the backdrop to major productions at the school, but also took it outside to places such as Southwark Cathedral.

Alan's reputation as a harpsichordist was growing too. As well as being tutor at Goldsmith's College, he played in groups such as the Praetorius Consort, the Noyse of Musicians, the Hanart Ensenble, and his big break really came when he was asked to be resident keyboard player in the famous international Consort of Musicke. Along with countless recordings and broadcasts, this group took Alan all over Europe and the UK with celebrity concerts, led by the inspiring Tony Rooley, and accompanying famous singers, notably Emma Kirkby.

The organ also became a major tool for Alan. Although brought up as a Baptist, his RCM days were dominated by visits to Westminster Abbey and St. Paul's Cathedral, and it was the Anglican tradition and liturgy that he was destined to follow.

After spells at St. John's Merton and St. Mary's Potters Bar, out of an application of a hundred candidates, he was appointed Director of Music and Organist at the London University Church of Christ the King. One of the main remits of this post was to provide music for a talented choir, drawn up of students from the various colleges in the University, but also to mould this with participation of a 'singing' congregation.

This resulted in a very formative and productive time in Alan's compositional career – writing new pieces, subsequently to be published, that would embrace this need.

Out came Mass and Canticle settings, along with anthems, and the choir became famous outside the building of Christ the King, singing in many cathedrals in the UK, as well as touring Germany and Belgium. Germany also became a contributor to Alan's professional work as teacher, performer and composer, as further invitations were forthcoming, leading to a strong connection which exists to this day.

Another exciting break in Alan's teaching and 'animator' career came, when in 1976 he was appointed Director of Music at Queen Mary College, University of London. Here he led the music through many productions, serving under a number of Principals, and witnessing the growth of the College as it transformed itself from small East End roots to being one of the key players in the University network. This, along with Christ the King, inspired new compositions from Alan. Two major 'pinnacles' were the 1984 commission of the musical 'The Palace of Delights' and the 2000 Millenium inter faith cantata 'The Harmony of the Spheres (QMC being an important multi cultural college). He retired finally from this university in 2013.

A parallel major change to Alan's career came in 1986. He left Christ the King and was quickly appointed to be Organist and Director of Music at the famous Bow Bells Church of St. Mary-le-Bow, London. This is the church, where if born within the sound of Bow Bells, one is a true cockney! The church is also mentioned in connection with 'the great bell of Bow' in the nursery rhyme 'Oranges and Lemons', which later inspired an organ composition from Alan based on these bells (which can now be heard on You Tube!)

This piece has become a frequent request at weddings.

His 32 years at this prestigious place came to a sad end this year February 2018, when he formally retired. It had been a highly productive time here, both with directing a small professional choir in the gallery and playing the organ, and of course composing new pieces for this genre. Perhaps though, the chief legacy Alan left at this church was, along with the driving force of the Rector, the Reverend George Bush, to campaign for a new organ resulting in the absolutely exquisite new Kenneth Tickell instrument installed in 2010 to replace a very bad Rushworth and Dreaper post war heap of badly put together pipes. To quote one person's subsequent comment, 'we have gone from having the worst organ in London to perhaps one of the best'. It certainly is a much sought after instrument, and many people are requesting to come in and give recitals.

Alongside appointments at Christ the King, QMC, St Mary-le-Bow, and tours with the Consort of Musicke, Alan has freelanced with other assignments. Most notably is his connection with the BBC, especially in directing, composing for and playing for Radio 4's long running Daily Service, resulting in intermittent trips to Manchester.

He was awarded an Honorary Associateship of the Royal School of Church Music in 2010, for services and achievements rendered – especially for his long standing contribution with the Sunday by Sunday team recommending appropriate music for Sunday worship sent out regularly to all the churches. He retired from this post too a couple of years ago.

At this time of writing, Alan is officially now retired from all his 'formal' posts. But music still goes on, as he embarks on a new phase in the journey. He still gives organ recitals around the country and has continued a close connection with Germany. Compositions are abundant, both new and the recycling of older ones.

There are however two major assignments which now have taken shape, and both are to do with serving local communities. They are poignant to Alan, being his two homes referred to earlier in this article.

He lives in a place called Sidcup, which, as well as being in the London Borough of Bexley, has as its postal address 'Kent', making this a desirable link between city and countryside. It is a very attractive 'green' area, and the neighbouring old town of Eltham (part of Greenwich) has at the top end of the town a fine Victorian building and flourishing community under the name of Holy Trinity. After retiring from St Mary-le-Bow, Alan learned that they were currently without a Director of Music. Here is an unusually large choir, cathedral size organ, warm family church and superb liturgies - all on the doorstep, so as to speak, which Alan knows well. As well as being Director of Music there in the 1990's, he was invited back last year in an interregnum to steer them through Lent and Holy Week before a new appointment was made. Sadly the new man had to leave recently for health reasons creating this sudden vacuum. What amazing timing! And so subsequently, Alan has enthusiastically thrown himself into full musical leadership and organ playing there, which is clearly a vibrant step in the next chapter of his life's journey.

Last but certainly not least, refers to Alan's other home – Eastwood. Although his parents are now long gone, he still has some family left and friends there, and intends to visit this very special place as much as possible. He loves exploring the area on local walks, always recalling the beauty of the surrounding countryside, reliving local history and associations. He has 'bonded' himself to two societies – the D H Lawrence Society and the Haggs Farm Society.

Last year he was invited to give an organ recital at Greasley Parish Church, as part of the Lawrence Festival of Culture. This turned out to be not just an organ recital, even though the beautiful Greasley Country Church and organ were chosen. The theme was widened to centre on three great local people, namely D. H. Lawrence, Lord Byron and Eric Coates, alongside other local connections, and the whole programme was punctuated by contributions from local social historians and entrepreneurs, revealing an exciting and colourful history and tradition in this prized corner of Nottinghamshire. It also provided a springboard for further projects, to take place later this year. Along with visits to his family and friends, Alan will be undertaking forthcoming valuable research on all sorts of untouched history of the Eastwood area. Clearly the D. H. Lawrence connection is major, but there are so many other cultural aspects to develop, some of which have not been fully unearthed. Being a local lad, remembering Eastwood as it was in his formative childhood years, discovering family history, and of course loving Lawrence and sharing this with like minded people, is a huge magnetic pull for Alan. Every trip and visit to Eastwood is a trip through time as memories abound and new experiences are created.

Retirement is not about stopping and giving up, but it paves the way for freedom to explore new territories and these two community 'homes' are clearly signalling the direction Alan is going, whilst still enjoying trips around the country playing church organs. Having enjoyed a distinguished and variable career, this is now about coming home, but certainly not withdrawing.

So where is Alan's home of the future to be exactly? If he could afford it, he clearly would have two homes, but that is never going to happen. Having spent all of his professional life in London (apart from a short spell in Peterborough) it doesn't seem likely that he can uproot now, but his thoughts and imagination constantly turn to Eastwood.

The last words must come from Lawrence as they speak totally to Alan *"I know that view better than any in the world…….. That's the country of my heart!"*

Eastwood Writers Group, Poetry Competition Winner: 'Dawn Raffle' shares her beautiful winning entry with us

'Dreamflight'

No sense or reason in my dreams
I dip and soar and glide it seems
I am a cloud or a bird in flight
I am flying high and travelling light

I feel the sunlight on the wing
My eyes are keen they see all things
The vole that scampers in the field
Nesting birds are soon revealed

The rush of air the thrill of the kill
The caw of the crows diverts my will
I retreat and soar a speck in the sky
The vole safe in the field passes by

I am flying high and travelling light
Not a cloud or bird in flight
I dip soar and glide and it seems
No sense or reason in my dreams

Dawn Raffle.

❧

Also from Dawn

'TIME'

What is time?
We may call it
and use it, or perhaps

make it and take it.
We spend it, choose it
and sometimes we lose it.
We might waste it, save it
or simply ignore it.
We measure it, count it
juggle it and keep it.
Sometimes we fear it
while trying to find it.
Is it a minute an hour?
Or a day, month or year
or is it just
this moment we share?

Dawn Raffle.

Joseph Henry Flint D.C.M.

By Granddaughters: Pauline Larder (Moore)
and Rosemary Taylor (Healey)

Joseph Henry Flint was born on January 6th 1892 and died January 6th 1963 at the age of 71. Joseph followed in his father's footsteps, Moses and brother Charles, as a coal face worker, cutting and loosening coal with a pick (a coalminer hewer) or referred to in some pits as ragging.

In October 1914 Joseph joined up. In 1915 he was in France. Joseph Flint was in the Kings Royal Rifles (based at Winchester) as part of Kitchener's Second New Army: 11th (Service) Battalion, 59th Brigade, 20th (Light) Division. He won 'The Distinguished Conduct Medal.'

When he left the army in 1920 he was a Sergeant: R/4347 Sgt.Joseph Flint, 11th Battalion. He had been in every actionin which the 11th had taken part at Ypres, from Jan. to July 1916, taking part in many Patrols and Raids.

In 1915 on 21st July, landing at Boulogne, concentrating in the Saint Omer area, and then to Fleurbaix area for 'Trench Familiarisation.' In 1916 they were in action at the battle of Mount Sorrel on The Somme, The Battle of Delville Wood, Guillemont, Fleurs-Courcelette, Morval and The Battle of Le-Transloy. In 1917 again action during the German Retreat to the Hindenburg line. Battles: Langemarck, Menin Road Ridge, Polygon Wood,The Cambrai Operations. In 1918 they're fighting again at the Battle of Saint Quentin against the heavily defended Hindenburg Line, The Somme Crossings, Rosiers, engaging in fierce fighting in each battle. In all, Joseph Henry Flint was involved in 18 battles that we know of, but I'm sure there were many, many more unacounted for. At the Armistice, 11 a.m. Nov. 11th 1918 The Division was in the area: Bavay and Maubeuge. Demobilisation began 7th Jan. 1919.

When Joseph Flint left the army he was a sergeant, and had been awarded The British War Medal, the Victory Medal and The Distinguished Conduct Medal. In all, the 20th Light Division had suffered the loss of 35,470 men killed, wounded and missing.

Joseph was born to his father Moses, then aged 46 and to Mother Elizabeth aged 39. He had siblings: Rachel, Mary Millicent, Lottie, and Lilly, Charles and William.

Joseph married Elsie Wardle in Oct. 1914 at Eastwood Notts. They had five children: Albert, William, Nora, Lottie and Joseph. At some time they moved to 14 Princess Street Eastwood, where he raised his family with his wife Elsie and where they both died.

The medals from the pictures are The Distinguished Conduct Medal, which was established in 1854 by Queen Victoria, for gallantry in the field. It was last awarded in 1993.

After the first World War: 1914-1918, three medals were awarded to almost every serviceman who had served from 1914, 1915, they were: the British War medal, The Victory Medal and either the 1914 Star or the 1914-15 Star.

These three campaign medals were warmly known as : Pip, Squeak, and Wilfred, as known from the Daily Mirror newspaper comic strip of the time: Pip is the dog, Squeak is the penguin, and Wilfred is the baby rabbit.

Pauline Larder (Moore) Rosmary Taylor (Healey)

Joseph Henry Flint and his mother Elizabeth (nee Fletcher)

The Distinguished Conduct Medal

First instituted in 1854 as an award for distinguished service in the field for Warrant Officers, NCO's and lower ranks. All awards of the DCM were announced in the London Gazette, usually with a citation although awards made as part of the King's Birthday or New Year's honours do not always have one.

A very detailed reference is "Recipients of the Distinguished Conduct Medal 1914-1920" by R. W. Walker, published 1980. A veterans group, called the DCM League, existed after the war.

The recipient was allowed to use the initials DCM after their name.

Sgt. R4347 Joseph H Flint
11th Bn. Kings Royal Rifle Corps.
He took part in every Regimental action from July 1915.
He was at Ypres from January to July 1916 taking part
in many patrols at Saluumires on October 3rd and showed
able leadership of his platoon, assuming command when
the officer was killed

Joseph Flint

His Distinguished Conduct Medal
was awarded on 3rd June 1919.
The citation appeared in the London
Gazette on 11th March 1920.

Joseph with his wife: Elsie (nee Wardle)
They were married october 1914

A poem to mark this Centenary Anniversary year to the great war of 1914-18

A Soldier's Farewell
I'm sorry Ma, I've got to go
Lord Kitchener says he needs me...So
I'm not the bravest, or so bold
But a safe long life just turns me cold

If I should fall, don't cry, or shed a tear
Just tell 'em I was proud to serve…
I saw it through and held my nerve…

I'm Sorry Ma, my ink's run out…
We leave for France tomorrow night
Our Captain says, would you believe
We'll all be home by Christmas Eve!
You loving Jimmy…
(Harry Riley)

'Magical Memories'
Don Chambers

There are two things which I remember about our family holiday at Skegness in the summer of 1937.

In an amusement arcade I was amazed to see an 'African male, produce a continual supply of eggs from his mouth. At this time there was a side-show in a different arcade where a man performed in a lion's cage. Tragedy occurred one day when the lion mauled Harold Davidson (former Rector of Stiffkey, Norfolk) and he died two days later.

As an early war-time Christmas present from an aunt I received a box of conjuring tricks. I found the enclosed instructions dificult to follow and I gave the box to my best friend.

One Saturday afternoon in 1942 I ventured out on the local bus to Ilkeston where I visited Woolworth's store. I spent my pocket money on a book (Modern Conjuring by J C Cannell)

Back home I located a pack of cards and learnt the first trick in the book. Thus my hobby began. Woolworth stores often had a counter which sold tricks and jokes and i gradually began to build up a small collection. The Japanese egg-bag cost sixpence. Opportunities gradually developed to entertain family and friends.

During the war years (1939-1945) concerts were occasionally given at local churches and other venues. Eastwood Wellington Methodist Church had a talented concert party which included musical items, comedy and a 'Chinese' magician (Mr. Will Ball) I looked forward to seeing him perform locally and appreciated his explanation for me of how to perform the wine and water trick.

I liked his magic word (Sim Sala Bim) - a word used by Dante, the famous American illusionist on his British tours 1936-1939. Not until some years later did I learn that Mr. Ball was in fact my wife's great uncle.

At the church which I attended we always had a Sunday School Party. Sometimes I entertained but on one occasion we had a visit from prof. Kershaw of Ilkeston. For one of his tricks he produced several white mice which caused quite a stir when he brought them forward into the audience. He was in demand locally and had worked as an ambulance man at New England Colliery, Newthorpe which closed in 1937.

Special celebrations took place both nationally and locally to celebrate V J Day – the end of the war in the far east 1945. Amongst numerous other activities a variety show on Mansfield Road recreation ground in Eastwood included two magicians. Rajah Khan (a Long Eaton teacher) presented an Indian act and another man ate drinking glasses and razor blades.

In 1946 on my first visit to London I persuaded my uncle to exchange a proposed visit to the Tower for a visit to the renowned magic shop of Davenports. I purchased several items and became a regular mail-order customer.

In my teens I paid frequent visits to the Nottingham Empire and other theatres to see well known illusionists including Lyle, Dante and Kalanag. Whilst serving in the RAF in Essex I joined the Magic Circle (in 1950) and continued to see numerous illusionists.

When I see the boxes of tricks for sale in the larger shops I wonder which other children will become fascinated by their contents.

Don Chambers

Eastern Magic at the Wolsey Factory Kimbeley
Children's Christmas Party Dec. 1965

A Brief □□□□□□ as a Volunteer for St. John Ambulance:
Moorgreen Nursing Division from 1973 to 2007
By Marion Smith

Meetings were held at Dora Phillips Hall Girls' Centre. At the time of my joining St. John, Lily Rowley was the Superintendent and Alison Smith (nee Fox) was the Divisional Officer. It wasn't long before Lily had ordered my uniform and a first-aid manual.

Within six months I had passed in all the exams needed to be a qualified first-aider and caring for the sick members within St. John. We had to answer questions on first-aid, apply dressings and bandages, put someone in the recovery position and demonstrate resucitation. 'Pleased with myself, all went well and I had passed my first–aid exam. However, exams have changed a great deal since 1973, becoming much more intense. The next step was first-aid duty, going out into the community. I was quite nervous at first, but soon got over that hurdle. My first duty was the annual Moorgreen Show.

It was a big event to cover for Moorgreen Ambulance Men and the Nursing Division, I remember Sue Pollard opening the show and Harvey Smith show-jumping and many more celebrities.

We attended Eastwood Town Football Club, Summer Fayres, Show Jumping events and the list is endless. The duty I will never forget is Nottingham Forest Football Ground. The ambulance men were away for the weekend and the nursing ladies covered the duty. We had a mini-bus to take us, when we arrived the duty officer in charge told us which part of the pitch we would cover. I was asked to go to the dug-out. 'What on earth is the dug-out?' I asked. I soon found out, **it was the place of honour!** I was sitting on the bench, and told if any footballer was injured I had to run onto the pitch with the stretcher. I thought to myself 'I hope no one gets injured.'

Thankfully they didn't, but what an experience!

I started to climb the ladder, became the sergeant (wasn't I keen), also the Treasurer and my final role was Divisional Officer. This was an honour!

I enjoyed my role of teaching first-aid and caring for the sick to our nursing members.

Once a year Moorgreen Colliery paid for a weekend away at the Miners Holiday Camp Rhyl. The weekend included lectures, film shows and practice drill for the Sunday Church Parade through the town of Rhyl. We looked forward to these weekends. We'd meet up with other nursing divisions and would have an enjoyable time, thanks to Moorgreen Colliery.

We were proud to be wearing our uniforms and we all looked so immaculate.

In 2002 I had been nominated for the prestigious Serving Sister Award.

The award is for members who do voluntary work outside of the charity. The ceremony took place at The Grand Priory Church, Clerkenwell, London.

The award has to be sanctioned (approved) by her Majesty The Queen. It is in her name that I was invested as a member of The Order of St. John. The silver medal I received is the sign of man's redemption. **What a Memorable Day we had!**

Later in the year I was presented with The Eastwood Mayor's Certificate. Councillor Don Rowley was the current Mayor and he presented the award to me and other members of the community.

In 1997 I was asked if I would take on the role as Officer in charge of the Nursing Cadets, which I did. It was a totally different role and responsibility, and top of the agenda was that the cadets had to take their first-aid exam every year.

෨

'Without the support of my dear, late husband Maurice Smith, I wouldn't have been able to have given the amount of time I gave to St. John. Maurice, was also a member of Moorgreen Ambulance men. He used to say to me:
'You spend more time with St. John than you do with me!'

෨

Marion joined the Brigade in the 1970's as a Nursing Member. She has always been keen to attend duties and, as an enthusiastic member of the Division, always exceptionally smart, with a good knowledge of the rules. In 1985 she attained the position of Divisional Officer and also became Treasurer of the Division.

many of the Divisions activities both educational and social have been organised by Marion, a job she excels at.

Marion has spent many hours each year supporting and raising funds for both the Cadet and Adult Divisions, including spending hours collecting for flag days and applying to local authorities for grants. She always finds time to attend many duties and is a well known figure in the local community.

In 1998 with the sudden resignation of the Cadet officer, Marion stepped in to help run the Cadet Division, although the Cadets had been seriously run down and had only two Cadets attending regularly, she recruited a new potential officer and ran a recruitment campaign at local schools and shops. This had resulted in the Cadets now having a membership of twenty.

Much of the organisation of a Cadet enrolement service in 1999 was undertaken by Marion and two of the Cadets obtained first place in their first competition due to the excellent training given by Marion.

In the two decades-plus, that Marion has been a member of Moorgreen Division she has always performed all of her duties to the highest standards. Her commitment to the Brigade has never faulted and I have no hesitation in recommending her admission to the order as a Serving Sister.

Presentation Photographs reproduced by kind permission of Peter Jordan

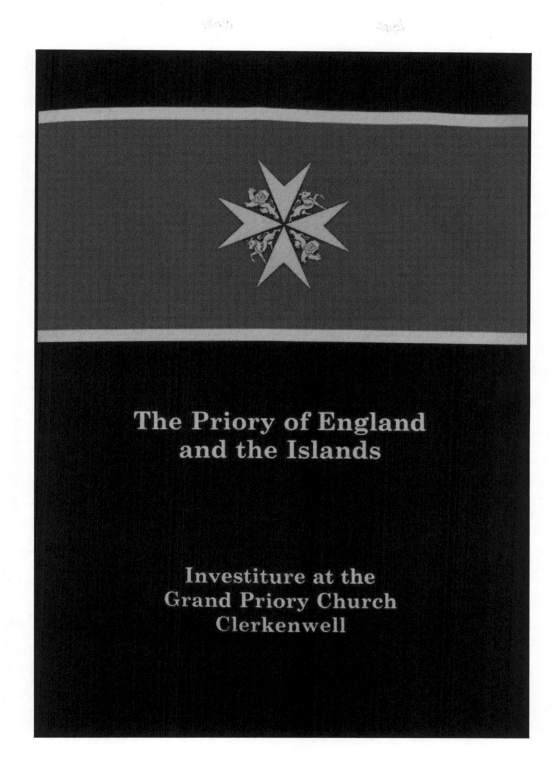

The Priory of England
and the Islands

Investiture at the
Grand Priory Church
Clerkenwell

Richard, Duke of Gloucester

Grand Prior of the Most Venerable Order of the Hospital of
St. John of Jerusalem, to

Marian, Mrs Smith

Greeting.

Whereas Her Majesty the Queen, the Sovereign Head of the Most Venerable Order of the Hospital of St. John of Jerusalem, has thought fit to sanction your appointment as a *Serving Sister* in the said Most Venerable Order.

Now therefore I, by these presents in the name and by the authority of Her Majesty do grant unto you the Dignity of a *Serving Sister* in the said Most Venerable Order, and I do hereby authorise you to have, hold and enjoy the said Dignity as a *Serving Sister* of the aforesaid Order, together with all and singular the privileges thereunto belonging or appertaining.

Given at St. John's Gate under the signature of His Royal Highness The Grand Prior and the seal of the said Most Venerable Order this Seventh day of December Two Thousand and One in the Forty Ninth year of Her Majesty's reign.

By the Grand Prior's Command

Chancellor

Grant of the Dignity of a Serving Sister
of the Most Venerable Order of the Hospital of St. John of Jerusalem to
Marian, Mrs Smith

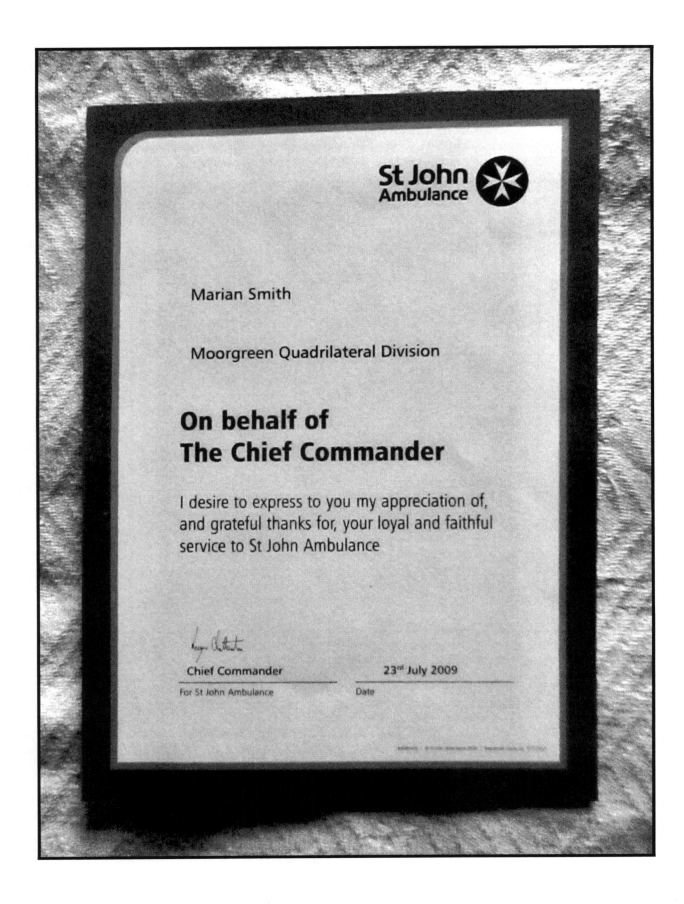

St John Ambulance
Nottinghamshire

St John
Ambulance

12 Park Drive
HUCKNALL
Nottingham
NG15 7LQ

20 July 2009

Mrs. M Smith
25 Garden Road
EASTWOOD
Nottingham
NG16 3FY

Dear Marion

RESIGNATION

Thank you for your recent letter tendering your resignation from the Brigade.

It is with a great deal of regret that I accept your resignation as I know how much you have put into the Cadets at Moorgreen over all the 30 years that you have been involved there. The hours of voluntary service that you have given, not only to the children but also the community of Eastwood, as a dedicated volunteer is much appreciated by many and I hope that you have many happy memories of your days in St John Ambulance.

I trust that you will be available to give help and advice if those that are continuing need it.

Once again many thanks for all that you have done for and the children and community of Eastwood, you have been a wonderful ambassador for St John Ambulance.

Regards

Eric Ridley
Commissioner
Trent Area

661 Valley Road
Basford
Nottingham NG5 1JG

T 0115 978 4625
F 0115 979 0163
www.sja.org.uk/notts

THE TOUCHWOOD CENTRE
4 CHARLOTTE STREET
ILKESTON
DERBYSHIRE
DE7 8LH

Tel. 01159 308947

Erewash Mental Health Association Limited is a Registered Charity, which has been in existence for over thirty years. Our Touchwood Centre is open every weekday from 10 am to 3.30 pm. There is no appointment system and no rationing of services.

Our aims are:

To provide a safe and supportive environment for adults with a diverse range of mental health issues, both long and short term.

To cater for individuals' specific needs.

To offer a range of therapeutic and social interactions in order to build confidence, facilitate independence and aid recovery.

To create an environment which encourages members to move forward through learning and adopting the life skills necessary to live, work and participate in their local community.

To encourage service receivers to be involved in the day to day running of the organisation by sharing their skills and experience with others giving them a sense of ownership and responsibility.

To offer refreshments and a nutritional lunch at a reasonable price.

To improve the quality of life for all our service receivers.

For more information visit:
www.touchwoodcentre.org.uk
Contact: Lesley Grand-Scrutton

Touchwood Premises

My name is David Coleman, born on the 22nd of September 1954, at 167 South street Eastwood, at my Grandmothers
house. My Grandmother's name was Irene Gertrude Crampton
but for some reason she was called Poppy or Pop.
My Mother's maiden name was Sheila Crampton.
My Fathers name was Valentine Coleman.
Sheila, my mam was the eldest of six, but my dad was the second
youngest of 22 (televisions weren't invented then)

Both have now passed away in the early 1990s

Well my dad kept up the tradition, I'm the eldest of nine, 6 sisters and 2 brothers. I can just remember living at 20 Moorfields Avenue Eastwood. As more of the family started to appear we moved to 81 Main street New Thorpe, my first school was Beauvale infants school, one of my memories was in the winter we had a open fire for heat in the class room and every now and again the care taker would come in and chuck a bucket of coal on the fire to keep it blazing.

More kids started to pop out so we moved again to number 56 New road Moorgreen. Turn left by the Horse and groom pub then about a mile later you come to four farm cottages on the left. The rent was 12/6p a week (just over 50p today) Well things went down hill from then on.

1. We had no water in the early mornings, or tea time, because the farmer needed all the available water for milking.
2. We didn't go to school much, my mam couldn't cope with us all, so I had to stay at home to help with whatever wanted doing, as my dad was a miner at Moorgreen pit.
3. No mobile shops would pass by, so if you wanted chicken the farmer would neck one for you. If you needed milk you took a billy can and again the farmer would fill it more or less straight from the cow.
4. The only way we could get to school was when the post man used to deliver to the farms around the area. We all got in the back of his van and he dropped us off near Beauvale school, we were sworn to secrecy not to tell any one as he would get into trouble.

5. On the way home from school (when we went) pit buses ran from Moorgreen pit to Watnall pit transferring miners'

back and forth, they used to stop and pick us up and drop us off at home.

6. The winter of 1963 was as bad as the north pole, snow drifted as high as the top of the hedges.
7. I could write a book about living up there, some other time perhaps.

Another baby arrived, so moved again, to number 12 Lindley Street, just off Engine lane, just below Moorgreen pit.
By then there was nine of us. About 60 yards away was a family of twelve kids, there must have been about 25 families
living there, on a summers evening when all the kids were out playing street games it was like moorgreen pit turning out at the end of the day shift. But still schooling was a low priority
for me, I must of missed about 60% of schooling out.

At the age of 15 I started at Moorgreen pit at the training centre, I stayed there until the age of 16. I started working
on the pit top working in various departments.

1. The joiners shop
2. The stock yard (learning how load underground supplies)
3. The shaft side (getting the supplies ready to go underground)
4. The pit top brick layers and so on until you went round the whole pit top.

It was only a laugh. When working with the pit top -
brick layers, at snap time they had their own cabin, when they started looking at each other, then all of a sudden they
pounced on me and had my trousers off and chucked me outside, trouserless. If that happened today they could have to go for therapy and then counselling.

Around the age of about 16 and ¾ I went underground working with a experienced miner under close personal supervision, same routine as the pit top, basically getting some pit sense.

If you want to know more about my underground escapades
You will have to read my book.
A Nottinghamshire pitmans' story,
David Coleman.
Published by Dayglo books.
Available from Amazon £8.99

At the age of nearly 18 I went into the army for 6 years,
serving in Northern Ireland twice, Cypress three times
2 united nation tours, 1 emergency tour, because the Greeks
And Turks had a go at each other. Tour in Germany and Belgium,
and of course England. A lot of experienced gained.
Another book one day.

After the army, back to Moorgreen pit as a coal bagger.
We had to deliver 14 tons of coal a day, but had to load it first
by hand, each bag weighing one hundred weight, or 50 kilo's
It's the sort of work that would kill a horse never mind a man.

Then after coal bagging I worked on pit tips driving huge earth movers, bull dozers and loading shovels.

The Strike, the only thing I have to say, that it shouldn't have happened in the first place. Arthur Scargill and Margaret Thatcher had their own agenda's.

As the coal industry went into decline I went back down the pit at Thorsby colliery north of the county. At Thorsby I was trained in mine ventilation, which the coal board sent me to college to get qualified (I passed)

I applied to join the mines rescue service. I passed all the medical tests and harsh training to become a fully qualified rescue man. I was now a team member of the Thoresby colliery rescue team.

I forgot to mention earlier, I was also in the territorial army which I served for 10 years.

6th of March 1991 I was trapped underground in a horrendous accident which you can read about in my book.

I was in the Queens medical hospital for nine weeks, then I was sent to Cedars physio hospital for 7 months.

Thus my mining career and territorial army came to a sudden end.

I now perform a one man show about coal miners, possibly the only one in the country that does it like I do. It has created a lot of media attention in the past. All done for worthwhile charities, mainly for 'When You Wish Upon A Star'.

I worked at the Q.M.C. for 25 years as a volunteer, 18 years of that was in accident and emergency.

The God given gift of healing came my way, so I embraced it with both hands, I've helped 100s of people in the past, with no complaints. That was 25 years ago. I have nothing against the medical profession at all, but if they would accept what I do, working together there is a lot more can be achieved.

I'm not particularly religious, but I feel a very spiritual man.

All for now me ducks, See you around Eastwood some time.

I do frequent the White Peacock Café a couple of times a week, the snap is lovely.

David Coleman. The Eastwood Pit man.

David Coleman with the Hairy Bikers (at pit)

□□□□e□ **Priory**

In book two we featured The history of Felley Priory Gardens Underwood Nottm. NG16 (Priory house not open to the public.) Nursery Tea Rooms and open times. It is still one of the regions best kept secrets and a '**must visit**' if you are in the area and can find the time, not least for it's beautifully kept gardens.

www.felleypriory.co.uk